Great Meals in Minutes

Wok Menus

This edition published 1995 by Bloomsbury Books, an
imprint of The Godfrey Cave Group, 42 Bloomsbury Street,
London, WC1B 3QJ.

ISBN 1 85471 528 3

Printed and bound in Great Britain.

Wok Menus

Ken Hom
Menu 1
Chicken Thighs with Garlic, Scallion,
  and Vinegar Sauce   8
Stir-Fried Squash with Szechwan Peppercorns
Fried Rice with Ham, Egg, and Peas

Menu 2
Cauliflower with Hoisin Sauce   10
Crisp Chicken Strips with Black-Bean Orange Sauce
Stir-fried Cucumbers with Tomatoes and Garlic

Menu 3
Chicken and Watercress Soup   12
Steamed Fish with Ginger, Scallions, and Coriander
Glazed Carrots with Oyster Sauce

Jane Philips
Menu 1
Hot and Sour Soup   16
Fried Chinese Turnip Cakes
Stir-Fried Shark with Chinese Cabbage and Noodles

Menu 2
Water Chestnut Fritters   18
Orange-Fried Beef
Broccoli-Studded Prawns/Rice

Menu 3
Shanghai Scallop Soup with 20 Garlic Cloves   21
Loin and Liver in Yellow Bean Sauce
Parcels of Spring Vegetables with Lemon Butter

Karen Lee
Menu 1
Chili Shrimp   26
Smoked Bean Sprouts
Diced Chicken with Fermented Black Beans

Menu 2
Orange Chicken   28
Stir-Fried Sugar Snap Peas
Stir-Fried Spinach with Fermented Bean Curd

Menu 3
Barbecued Lamb   31
Sautéed Green Beans, Szechwan Style
Braised Turnips with Black Mushrooms

John Bentley
Menu 1
Four-Season Dumplings with Sweet-and-Sour Sauce   36
Stir-Fried Vegetables with Shredded Lamb
Eight-Treasure Noodles with Chinese Sausage

Menu 2
Nest of the Phoenix   38
Spring Vegetable Stir-Fry
South-East Asian Beef Noodles

Menu 3
Tofu with Sweet Pepper and Peanuts, Szechwan-Style   40
Stir-Fried Vegetables in a Sweet-and-Sour Sauce
Stir-Fried Chinese Cabbage and Plantain

Mai Leung
Menu 1
Spinach and Egg Shred Soup   44
Diced Chicken, Szechwan Style
Stir-Fried Green Beans with Garlic

Menu 2
Five-Fragrance Oyster Fritters   46
Steamed Sesame Aubergine
Jade-Green Broccoli

Menu 3
Pork Shreds and Szechwan Pickle Soup   48
Beef and Scallops with Oyster Sauce
Stir-Fried Snow Peas with Mushrooms and Almonds

Francis Morton
Menu 1
Rice Congée   54
Warm Szechwan Noodles with Spiced Beef
Lamb and Broccoli Stir-Fry

Menu 2
Hot and Sweet Soup with Seafood Dumplings   56
Shining Noodle Salad with Beef and Tomato
Nonya Rice Noodles with Prawns

Menu 3
Stir-Fried Pork with Mange-Tout   58
Ma Po Szechwan Noodles
Steamed Chinese Cabbage with Green Pepper

Bloomsbury Books
London

Ken Hom

Menu 1

(Left)

Chicken Thighs with Garlic,
Scallion, and Vinegar Sauce
Stir-Fried Squash
with Szechwan Peppercorns
Fried Rice with Ham, Egg, and Peas

Ken Hom, born in Arizona and now based in California, learned to cook twenty-two years ago in his uncle's Chinese restaurant in Chicago. Most of the chefs there came from Hong Kong, and Ken Hom still relies on the Southern Chinese tastes and techniques that he learned in his early training. But he also had the chance to serve as an apprentice to cooks from other regions – Shanghai, Peking, and the Western provinces of Szechwan and Hunan – who were specialists in highly spiced foods long before most restaurants here began serving them.

From his Chicago experience, Ken Hom also learned the virtues of improvisation. Following recipes to the letter, he says, is not nearly as important as starting with fresh ingredients. If a recipe calls for fish and you cannot find any fresh fish, you are better off substituting boned chicken breasts than using frozen fish. If a recipe calls for special ingredients that are impossible to find, use something else. Above all, trust your instincts.

The three menus here achieve classic Chinese tastes with familiar Western ingredients. Menu 2 features cauliflower, a vegetable not even available in China. Menus 1 and 3 have the abundance of vegetables typical of Cantonese cooking. Common to these three meals is a range of contrasting textures.

In this satisfying meal, the colours of the squash and peppers add a festive note. A green or yellow platter for the fried rice will pick up the colours of the scrambled eggs or the green peas. The chicken thighs look appetizing on a bed of lettuce.

Chicken Thighs with Garlic, Scallion, and Vinegar Sauce
Stir-Fried Squash with Szechwan Peppercorns
Fried Rice with Ham, Egg, and Peas

This meal of chicken thighs, stir-fried squash, and fried rice is ideal family fare. The garlic-laden chicken thighs are the star attraction, a spicy dish to accompany the milder fried rice. Garlic is a Chinese favourite, and in this dish, it is spooned over the chicken in a soy and vinegar sauce.

Szechwan peppercorns, unlike the familiar black peppercorns, are tiny reddish-brown kernels covered with a husk. They taste mildly hot and have a pungent aroma. To heighten their flavour, cook the peppercorns for a few moments in an ungreased pan over a medium flame. Shake the pan frequently so that the kernels do not burn. When they have released their aromatic oil, remove them from the heat and allow them to cool slightly. Then grind them in a blender or coffee mill. Store the unused portion in a tightly covered jar.

The crushed peppercorns are used to season the stir-fried vegetables. Courgettes and yellow squash are most plentiful in the summer but are nonetheless available all year. For the tenderest squash, buy those that are less than 20 cm (8 inches) long. Sweet red bell peppers should be firm and shiny.

A platter of fried rice is a Cantonese speciality; indeed, it can easily be a meal in itself. In making fried rice, which is a staple of home-style cooking, you can be flexible about what you add to the dish. Before stir-frying, start with cold and firm cooked rice so that the grains will stay separate when you do stir-fry. Ham, eggs, and peas are the ingredients in this recipe, but you may also add nuts, cooked cubed chicken, cooked shrimp, mushrooms – or almost any good leftover vegetables or meats. The eggs, of course, are as essential as the rice, and peas or a green vegetable add a pleasing colour.

What to drink

Because of the prominence of the garlic and the peppercorns, beer would go especially well with this meal. However, if you are interested in experimenting, this menu provides an opportunity to match a red wine with Chinese food: first preference would be a light, fresh wine, like a Beaujolais or an inexpensive California Zinfandel.

Start-to-Finish Steps

1 Follow general rice recipe on page 9, steps 1 and 2.
2 Follow chicken recipe steps 1 and 2.
3 Mince the scallions and garlic for the chicken recipe and follow step 3.
4 Trim prosciutto or ham and follow fried rice recipe steps 1 to 4.
5 Follow stir-fried squash recipe step 1.
6 Follow fried rice recipe step 5.
7 Follow stir-fried squash recipe step 2.
8 Follow chicken recipe steps 4 to 6.
9 Follow general rice recipe step 3 and fried rice recipe steps 6 and 7. Remove to heatproof serving platter and keep warm.
10 Wipe out pan. Follow chicken recipe steps 7 and 8.
11 Wipe out pan. Follow stir-fried squash recipe steps 3 to 5.
12 Remove stir-fried rice and chicken from oven. Garnish chicken recipe as in step 9 and serve everything at once.

Chicken Thighs with Garlic, Scallion, and Vinegar Sauce

1½ kg (3 lbs) chicken thighs
60 g (2 oz) finely minced scallion
3 level tablespoons minced garlic (about 6 cloves)
4 tablespoons Chinese red rice vinegar, or 3 tablespoons Western red wine vinegar
4 tablespoons light soy sauce
1 ltr (1¾ pts) peanut oil
Curly endive or lettuce for garnish (optional)

1 Bring 2½ cm (1 inch) of water to a boil in wok or in large skillet.
2 Place chicken on heatproof platter and set on metal trivet or rack to steam, covered, 20 minutes.
3 Combine scallion, garlic, vinegar, and soy sauce in small bowl.
4 Preheat oven to SLOW.
5 Heat wok, add oil, and heat to 190°C (375°F) on deep-fat thermometer or until a scallion ring sizzles on contact.

6 Remove chicken from steamer and blot any moisture on the thighs with paper towels.

7 Gently add half the chicken pieces to the hot oil and deep-fry until crisp and brown, about 10 minutes.

8 Remove chicken thighs with Chinese mesh spoon or long-handled slotted metal spoon and briefly hold them above pan to drain off excess oil. Arrange them on large platter and keep warm in oven. Return oil to 190°C (375°F) and cook second batch. Keep warm in oven.

9 Serve chicken on bed of lettuce, if desired, and spoon over some of the vinegar sauce. Serve remaining sauce separately.

Stir-Fried Squash with Szechwan Peppercorns

1 teaspoon Szechwan peppercorns
350 g (12 oz) yellow squash (about 2 medium size)
350 g (12 oz) courgettes (about 2 medium size)
2 red bell peppers, seeded and cored
3 tablespoons peanut oil
2 teaspoons salt

1 Cook peppercorns in dry wok or small skillet over medium heat about 1 minute. Spin them in blender only until crushed and set aside.

2 Thinly slice squash and courgettes on the bias. Slice peppers into thin strips.

3 Heat wok until it takes on a rainbowlike shimmer or heat large, heavy skillet. Add peanut oil.

4 When oil is almost smoking, add salt and sliced squash and courgette. Stir-fry quickly over high heat, then immediately add red peppers. Stir-fry until vegetables are slightly wilted, about 3 minutes.

5 Stir in crushed peppercorns and toss well to combine. Spoon onto serving platter and keep warm.

Fried Rice with Ham, Egg, and Peas

125 g (4 oz) proscuitto in one piece and trimmed of fat
4 large eggs
1 teaspoon sesame oil
1 teaspoon salt
125 g (4 oz) fresh peas, shelled
4 tablespoons peanut oil
750 g (1½ lb) cooked rice, at room temperature

1 Cut ham into 5 mm (¼ inch) cubes.

2 Bring 125 ml (4 fl oz) water to a boil in small saucepan.

3 Beat eggs with chopsticks or a fork and add sesame oil and salt.

4 Cook peas in boiling water 3 minutes. Drain in colander.

5 Heat large heavy skillet until almost smoking. Add 1 tablespoon of the oil. Add egg mixture and stir-fry until partially 'set' in one piece. Turn out onto small plate and slice into thin strips. Set aside.

6 Wipe out pan with paper towels and reheat. Add remaining 3 tablespoons oil. When almost smoking, add rice and ham. Cook, stirring constantly to prevent sticking, about 5 minutes, or until rice is thoroughly heated.

7 Add cooked eggs and peas, and heat, stirring, 3 to 5 minutes. Taste for seasoning.

Added touch

Perfect Rice

500 ml (1 pt) cold water
250 g (8 oz) raw long-grain rice

1 Add the water and rice to a medium-size saucepan. Heat uncovered until water comes to a full boil.

2 Turn heat to low and cover. Simmer rice for 20 minutes without stirring.

3 Remove pot from heat and let it stand 5 to 10 minutes.

4 Remove cover and fluff rice with a fork before serving.

Cauliflower with Hoisin Sauce
Crisp Chicken Strips with Black-Bean Orange Sauce
Stir-fried Cucumbers with Tomatoes and Garlic/Rice

Crisp strips of chicken and cauliflower florets glazes with hoisin sauce provides a pretty colour contrast to the stir-fried cucumbers with tomatoes and garlic. Use informal pottery for this appealing one-plate meal.

The rich spicy *hoisin* sauce adds a pleasant nutty colour and brings out the slightly cabbagey taste of crisp-cooked cauliflower in the first dish of this menu.

The stir-fried chicken has a sauce flavoured with salted black beans, garlic, and orange juice. Salted black beans are soy beans that have been boiled and then soaked in brine for six months

The zest of an orange is its outer skin, shaved off without the underlying white rind. When you mince or grate the zest, the oils in it will release a wonderful fragrance.

What to drink
Serve a robustly flavoured tea such as China Green or Keemum or, if you want wine, a California Chenin Blanc.

Start-to-Finish Steps
1 Follow chicken recipe step 1. Preheat oven to SLOW.
2 Follow stir-fried cucumbers recipe step 1.
3 Follow chicken recipe steps 2 to 5.
4 Trim cauliflower into florets, mince scallions, and follow cauliflower recipe steps 1 to 3.
5 Follow stir-fried cucumbers recipe steps 2 and 3.
6 Follow chicken recipe steps 6 and 7.
7 Follow cauliflower recipe step 4. Keep cauliflower warm in oven while you cook the cucumbers.
8 Wipe out pan. Follow stir-fried cucumbers recipe steps 4 to 6. Remove chicken from oven and follow step 8. Remove cauliflower from oven and serve.

Cauliflower with Hoisin Sauce

1 level tablespoon salt
1 head cauliflower (about 750 g (1½ lb))
6 tablespoons *hoisin* sauce
1 tablespoon sesame oil
3 level tablespoons minced scallions

1 Bring 500 ml (1 pt) water to a boil in large saucepan. Add salt and blanch cauliflower 5 minutes.

2 Mix remaining ingredients in small bowl.
3 Drain cauliflower in colander and let cool 5 minutes.
4 Turn into serving bowl and toss with sauce mixture.

Crisp Chicken Strips with Black-Bean Orange Sauce

The chicken marinade:
750 g-1 kg (1½ to 2 lb) skinless, boneless chicken breasts
2 eggs
2 tablespoons peanut oil
2 tablespoons dark soy sauce
1 tablespoon Chinese rice wine or dry sherry
½ teaspoon sugar

The deep frying:
1 ltr (1¾ pts) peanut oil
60-100 g (2-3 oz) unbleached flour
60-100 g (2-3 oz) cornstarch

The sauce:
2 tablespoons peanut oil
2 tablespoons Chinese salted black beans
2 tablespoons minced garlic (about 6 cloves)
125 ml (4 fl oz) Chinese Chicken stock
60 ml (2 fl oz) freshly squeezed orange juice
1 level tablespoon cornstarch dissolved in 3 tablespoons water
1 teaspoon Chinese sesame oil
Orange zest for garnish (optional)

1 Cut chicken into long strips about 2½ cm (1 inch) wide. Combine marinade ingredients in medium-size bowl and blend well. Add chicken strips, tossing to coat them with marinade.
2 Heat peanut oil in wok or 190°C (375°F) on deep-fat thermometer or until a sliver of garlic sizzles.
3 Combine flour and cornstarch in medium-size bowl. Coat chicken strips in the mixture, shaking off any excess.
4 Deep-fry the strips in two batches until they are golden brown, about 3 to 5 minutes. Remove them with Chinese mesh spoon or long-handled slotted metal spoon and drain them over pan. Place on platter lined with paper towels and keep warm in oven.
5 Drain wok, and wipe out with paper towels.
6 For the sauce, heat wok until it takes on a rainbowlike shimmer or heat large heavy skillet until almost smoking. Add 2 tablespoons peanut oil, then black beans and garlic. Stir-fry 30 seconds.
7 Add chicken stock and orange juice, and bring to

a boil. Stir in cornstarch mixture and cook, stirring constantly, until thickened and bubbling. Add sesame oil and remove from heat. Pour sauce into serving bowl.
8 Pour a little of the sauce over the chicken strips and garnish with orange zest, if desired. Serve remaining sauce on the side.

Stir-fried Cucumbers with Tomatoes and Garlic

3 large cucumbers (about 750 g (1½ lb))
2 teaspoons salt
4 large tomatoes (about 750 g (1½ lb))
2 tablespoons sugar
2 tablespoons peanut oil
3 level tablespoons minced shallots
2 level tablespoons minced garlic (about 6 cloves)
2 teaspoons sesame oil

1 Peel cucumbers and cut in half lengthwise. Scoop out seeds with teaspoon. Cut cucumber halves into long strips, then crosswise into 2½ cm (1 inch pieces). Put in colander and sprinkle with 1 teaspoon of salt.
2 Bring 1 ltr (1¾ pts) water to a boil in large saucepan. Blanch tomatoes, 2 at a time, 10 seconds. Peel, seed, and chop tomatoes. Put in medium-size bowl and sprinkle with sugar.
3 Remove cucumbers and blot with linen kitchen towel or paper towels. Drain chopped tomatoes in colander.
4 Heat wok until it takes on a rainbowlike shimmer or heat large heavy skillet and add peanut oil.
5 Add cucumber to the hot oil and stir to coat. Add shallots, garlic, remaining 1 teaspoon salt and sesame oil. Stir-fry 3 minutes.
6 Add tomatoes and toss just to warm, about 1 minute. Serve immediately.

<table>
<tr><td>

Menu

3
</td><td>

Chicken and Watercress Soup
Steamed Fish with Ginger, Scallions, and Coriander
Glazed Carrots with Oyster Sauce/Rice
</td></tr>
</table>

You can serve this informal meal in the various cooking containers – a copper pot, a bamboo steamer, and a wok.

This light, nutritious meal of soup, steamed fish, glazed carrots, and rice makes a fine warm-weather luncheon or dinner. The delicate homemade chicken soup is flavoured with pieces of chicken strained from the broth. To prepare the stock Western-style, disjoint the chicken and add the pieces to the boiling water. Or, you may prepare the stock by the authentic Chinese method of cleaving the chicken into two-inch pieces, which exposes more chicken surface and produces a richer chicken flavour. The watercress also adds its good tart flavour. You put the fresh leaves in the soup bowl – not in the pot – and pour the broth over them. This gently blanches and wilts the watercress but does not overcook it.

Use any of the fish the recipe calls for as long as they are fresh. The carrots provide an unusual flavour when combined with the oyster sauce.

What to drink
Because of its simplicity, this menu will accommodate a dry, relatively full-bodied white wine, such as a moderately priced Californian or New World Chardonnay.

Start-to-Finish Steps
1   Follow chicken soup recipe steps 1 to 3.
2   Preheat oven to SLOW. Follow glazed carrots recipe step 1.

3   Follow chicken soup recipe steps 4 and 5.
4   Slice ginger for chicken soup recipe; mince ginger for steamed fish recipe. Follow general rice recipe on page 9, steps 1 and 2.
5   Follow steamed fish recipe steps 1 to 3.
6   Follow glazed carrots recipe step 2.
7   Follow rice recipe step 3 and chicken soup recipe step 6.
8   Follow glazed carrots recipe step 3.
9   Follow chicken soup recipe steps 7 and 8, steamed fish recipe step 4, rice recipe step 4, and serve.

Chicken and Watercress Soup

1¼ kg (2½ lb) whole chicken
350-500 g (¾ -1 lb) skinless, boneless chicken breasts
4 thin slices fresh ginger
4 scallions, white part only
Salt
100 g (3 oz) loosely packed fresh watercress leaves

1   Bring 2 ltrs (4½ pts) water to a boil in stockpot or kettle.
2   Using heavy cleaver or knife, disjoint whole

chicken or, to prepare Chinese style, chop into 5 cm (2 inch) pieces.

3 Separately, cut boneless chicken breasts into short, thin strips.

4 Blanch chicken breast strips in the boiling water 1 minute. Remove with Chinese mesh spoon or slotted metal spoon to heatproof plate and keep warm in preheated slow oven.

5 Add the cut-up chicken to the boiling water. Turn down heat and skim off any scum that forms on surface. Add ginger, scallions, and salt to taste, and simmer, uncovered, about 30 minutes, skimming from time to time. The broth should be reduced by half.

6 Ten minutes before serving, strain broth through sieve lined with cheesecloth into large bowl to remove chicken pieces, ginger, and scallions used for flavouring. Rinse out pot. Using your spoon or a triple layer of paper toweling gently draped across the surface, remove surface fat from broth. Reserve 250 ml (8 fl oz) for glazed carrots.

7 Return remaining broth and blanched chicken strips to pot. Reheat and add salt if necesary.

8 Place handful of watercress leaves into each of four soup bowls. Ladle hot broth and chicken pieces into the bowls.

Glazed Carrots with Oyster Sauce

1 kg (2 lb) baby carrots
1 tablespoon peanut oil
2 cloves garlic, peeled and lightly crushed
250 ml (8 fl oz) reserved chicken broth from soup recipe or canned broth
2 tablespoons oyster sauce

1 Peel carrots and roll cut them.

2 Heat wok until it has a rainbowlike shimmer or heat large, heavy skillet until almost smoking and add peanut oil. Add carrots and crushed garlic. Stir quickly with 2 wooden spoons to coat carrots with a thin film of oil.

3 Add broth and oyster sauce, and cook over high heat 10 minutes. The liquid should be reduced almost to a glaze. Stir carrots from time to time to be sure they are evenly glazed. Remove from heat and turn into serving bowl.

Steamed Fish with Ginger, Scallions, and Coriander

4 fresh halibut or sea bass steaks (about 750 g (1$\frac{1}{2}$ lbs)
Salt and freshly ground pepper
1 level tablespoon minced scallions
1 level tablespoon minced coriander
1 teaspoon minced fresh ginger
1$\frac{1}{2}$ tablespoons peanut oil

1 Bring 2$\frac{1}{2}$ cm (1 inch) of water to a boil in wok or small roasting pan.

2 Place fish steaks on heatproof platter and set on rack or metal trivet. Sprinkle fish with salt and pepper, and scatter scallions, coriander, and ginger over them.

3 If using wok, cover with wok lid. If using roasting pan, cover tightly with double-strength aluminium foil. Steam fish steaks 8 to 12 minutes, depending on their thickness, or until done. Be careful of the hot steam, particularly if you are lifting up tent of aluminium foil.

4 Just before serving, heat peanut oil in small saucepan. Drizzle over the steamed fish.

Jane Philips

Menu 1
(Left)
Hot and Sour Soup
Fried Chinese Turnip Cakes
Stir-Fried Shark with Chinese Cabbage and Egg Noodles

Jane Philips was converted to the pleasure of Wok cookery at an early stage in her cooking career. 'For quick, one-pot cookery it really cannot be beaten,' she says. 'The scope for experimentation with flavours and textures is endless.

A great lover of Chinese food, she has picked up many tips and ideas for her recipe collection from restaurants around the country, adding variations to suit her own tastes and to adapt to availability of produce. While not being necessarily traditional Chinese fare, all her menus have a distinct Chinese flavour to them.

The Chinese Turnip Cakes in Menu 1 are more time-consuming than most recipes in this book, but the loaf may be cooked in advance, leaving the frying of the cakes until the meal is almost ready. They make a delicious accompaniment to the pungent Hot-and-Sour Soup.

The soups in Menus 1 & 3, bursting with flavour, are simple to prepare but allow time to stir-fry the other dishes.

Hot and sour soup, fried Chinese turnip cakes and almond milk with apricots.

<table>
<tr><td rowspan="3">

</td><td>

Hot and Sour Soup
Fried Chinese Turnip Cakes
Stir-Fried Shark with Chinese Cabbage and Egg Noodles

</td></tr>
</table>

What to drink

With the fish and the Turnip Cakes a dry clean white such as Muscadet Sir Lie would be suitable.

Start-to-Finish Steps

1   The night before, follow turnip cakes recipe steps 1 to 4.
2   Gather together and prepare the ingredients for shark and hot and sour soup recipes. Follow shark recipe step 1.
3   Follow soup recipe steps 1 and 2 and turnip cakes recipe steps 5 and 6. Keep both warm while you prepare the shark dish.
4   Follow shark recipe steps 2 to 5.
5   Serve soup and turnip cakes, keeping shark dish warm until ready to serve.

Hot and Sour Soup

1¹/₂ ltrs (2¹/₂ pts) unsalted chicken stock
4 tablespoons rice vinegar
2 tablespoons Chinese black vinegar or balsamic vinegar
1 to 2 tablespoons chili paste with garlic, or 5 to 10 drops Tabasco sauce
1 tablespoon low-sodium soy sauce or shoyu
1 tablespoon dry sherry
¹/₂ teaspoon finely chopped garlic
1 to 2 teaspoons finely chopped fresh ginger root
1 carrot julienned
6 dried shiitake or Chinese black mushrooms, covered with boiling water and soaked for 20 minutes, stemmed, the caps thinly sliced
15 g (¹/₂ oz) cloud-ear mushrooms (optional), covered with boiling water and soaked for 20 minutes, thinly sliced
175 g (6 oz) bamboo shoots (optional), rinsed and julienned
2 tablespoons cornflour, mixed with 3 tablespoons water
250 g (8 oz) firm tofu (bean curd), cut into thin strips
3 spring onions, trimmed and sliced diagonally into ovals

1   Heat the stock in a large pan over medium-high heat. Add the rice vinegar, Chinese black vinegar, chili paste ot Tabasco sauce, soy sauce, sherry,

finely chopped garlic and ginger, julienned carrot and sliced shiitake or Chinese black mushrooms, and, if you are using them, the sliced cloud-ear mushrooms and bamboo shoots.
2   Bring the liquid to the boil, then stir in the cornflour mixture. Reduce the heat and simmer the soup, stirring, until it thickens slightly – 2 to 3 minutes. Gently stir in the tofu. Ladle the soup into bowls and garnish each serving with the spring onion slices.

Fried Chinese Turnip Cakes

750 g (1¹/₂ lb) white turnip, or daikon radish, (mooli) peeled and coarsely grated
125 ml (4 fl oz) unsalted chicken stock
75 g (2¹/₂ oz) plain flour
15 g (¹/₂ oz) dried shrimps, finely chopped
¹/₂ sweet red or green pepper, seeded, deribbed and finely diced
2 egg whites, lightly beaten
2 teaspoons rice vinegar or distilled white vinegar
¹/₄ teaspoon salt
freshly ground black pepper
2 teaspoons safflower oil

1   Pour enough water into a large saucepan to fill it about 2¹/₂ cm (1 inch) deep. Set a vegetable steamer in the pan and bring the water to the boil. Put the turnip into the steamer, cover the pan and reduce the heat to medium low. Steam the turnip until it is very tender – about 15 minutes. While the turnip is cooking, blend the chicken stock and flour in a 2 ltr (3¹/₂ pt) saucepan to form a smooth paste.
2   Drain the turnip in a sieve, pressing it with the back of a wooden spoon to get rid of any excess water. Add the turnip to the flour paste and cook the mixture over low heat, stirring constantly for 3 minutes.
3   Remove the pan from the heat and stir in the dried shrimps, red or green pepper, egg whites, vinegar, salt, and one or two grindings of black pepper. Spoon the mixture into a lightly oiled 10 by 20 cm (4 by 8 inch) glass or enamelled loaf dish, smooth the top with the back of a spoon and cover the pan lightly with plastic film.

4 Place the loaf dish in a pan large enough to hold it and pour in 1 cm (¹/₂ inch) of water. Bring the water to the boil. Cover the pan, reduce the heat to medium low, and poach the loaf until it is firm to the touch – about 40 minutes. Remove the loaf dish from the pan and allow the loaf to cool completely. If you wish, it may be chilled overnight.

5 Loosen the loaf from the sides of the dish with a knife, then turn it out on to a cutting board. Cut the loaf into 5 mm (¹/₄ inch) slices.

6 Brush a large, non-stick frying pan with 1 teaspoon of the oil, then set the pan over medium-high heat. Add half of the turnip cake slices and sauté them, turning them once, until they are brown on both sides. Transfer the slices to a heated platter. Brush the pan with the remaining oil and brown the remaining slices in the same manner.

Stir-Fried Shark with Chinese Cabbage and Egg Noodles

500 g (1 lb) shark meat (or swordfish or tuna)
2 tablespoons low-sodium soy sauce or shoyu
1 tablespoon dark sesame oil
1 tablespoon fresh lime juice
1 bunch spring onions, trimmed, sliced diagonally into 1 cm (¹/₂ inch) pieces, the white parts kept separate from the green
2 garlic cloves, finely chopped
1 tablespoon orange marmalade or apricot jam
Freshly ground black pepper
1¹/₂ tablespoons safflower oil
1 carrot, peeled, halved lengthwise and cut diagonally into thin slices
500 g (1 lb) Chinese cabbage, trimmed and sliced into 2 cm (³/₄ inch) strips
500 g (1 lb) fresh Chinese egg noodles

1 Wash the fish under cold running water and pat it dry with paper towels. Cut it into pieces about 5 cm (2 inches) long and 1 cm (¹/₂ inch) wide. In a large bowl, combine 1 tablespoon of the soy sauce with the sesame oil, lime juice, white spring onion pieces, garlic, marmalade or jam and some pepper. Add the fish pieces to the mixture and let them marinate for at least 15 minutes.

2 Bring 4 ltrs (7 pts) water to a rolling boil over high heat.

3 In a wok or a large frying pan, heat 1 tablespoon of the safflower oil over high heat. Add the carrot slices and stir-fry them for 1 minute, then add the cabbage, all but 1 tablespoon of the green spring onion pieces and the remaining soy sauce. Stir-fry the vegetables until the cabbage is barely wilted – about 2 minutes. Transfer the vegetables to a bowl.

4 Add noodles to boiling water and cook until tender — about 3 minutes.

5 Heat the remaining safflower oil in the wok or pan over high heat. Add the marinated fish and gently stir-fry it until it is opaque and feels firm to the touch – approximately 2 minutes. Return the vegetables to the pan and toss them with the fish. Transfer the mixture to a large plate, sprinkle with the reserved green spring onion pieces, and arrange on a bed of egg noodles. Serve.

Added touch

Almond Milk with Apricots

2 packets powdered gelatine
350 ml (12 fl oz) semi-skimmed milk
6 tablespoons sugar
1 tablespoon almond extract
8 canned apricot halves, drained, rinsed if packed in syrup, and patted dry
1 tablespoon flaked almonds (optional)
1 tablespoon toasted desiccated coconut (optional)

1 Pour 125 ml (4 fl oz) of cold water into a bowl and sprinkle the gelatine on to the water. While the gelatine softens, bring ¹/₄ ltr (8 fl oz) of water to the boil, then pour it into the bowl, stirring to dissolve the gelatine. Add the milk, sugar and almond extract and stir to dissolve the sugar. Pour the mixture into a 20 cm (8 inch) square dish, and distribute the apricot halves in the mixture so that when the dessert is cut into squares each will contain an apricot half. Refrigerate the dessert until it is set – about 2 hours; the dessert may be kept in the refrigerator overnight.

2 To serve, cut the dessert into squares, place the squares on a serving platter and, if you like, top each with some of the almonds and coconut.

Menu 2	**Water Chestnut Fritters** **Orange-Fried Beef** **Broccoli-Studded Prawns/Rice**

What to drink
A light fruity red such as Beaujolais could well match the particular flavours of this menu.

Start-to-Finish Steps
1   Follow orange-fried beef recipe steps 1 to 3 and broccoli-studded prawns recipe steps 1 and 2.
2   Prepare and cook water chestnut fritters and keep them warm in a SLOW oven. Prepare dipping sauce and set aside.
3   Follow prawns recipe step 3 and general rice recipe on page 9 steps 1 and 2.
4   Follow beef recipe steps 4 to 7 and rice recipe steps 3 and 4. Serve.

Water Chestnut Fritters

500 g (1 lb) fresh water chestnuts
1 teaspoon sugar, dissolved in 1 ltr (1¹/₃ pts) cold water
90 g (3 oz) uncooked chicken breast meat, coarsely chopped
125 g (4 oz) mushrooms, stemmed
1 spring onion, trimmed and chopped
2 tablespoons finely chopped fresh ginger root
1 garlic clove, finely chopped
1 tablespoon low-sodium soy sauce, or naturally fermented shoyu
2 tablespoons peanutoil

Although canned water chestnuts may be used, fresh ones are sweeter and have more flavour.

18

Ginger-Garlic Dip
1 tablespoon finely chopped fresh ginger root
1 garlic clove, finely chopped
125 ml (4 fl oz) rice vinegar
1/2 teaspoon dark sesame oil
6 thin carrot rounds

1 Peel the water chestnuts with a small, sharp knife, and drop them into the sugared water as you work. (The sugar in the water will help preserve the water chestnuts' natural sweetness.)
2 Preheat the oven to 180°C (350°F or Mark 4). Put the chicken, mushrooms, spring onion, ginger, garlic and soy sauce in a food processor or blender. Purée the mixture, stopping occasionally to scrape down the sides, until it is smooth – about 4 minutes. Transfer the purée to a mixing bowl. Chop the chestnuts coarsely and combine them with the purée. With your hands, mould the mixture into balls about 2 1/2 cm (1 inch) in diameter (there will be 25 to 30 of these).
3 Heat the oil in a large, shallow fireproof casserole over medium-high heat. Brown the fritters on one side for about 2 minutes. Turn them over and put the casserole in the oven. Bake the fritters until they are browned and cooked through – 5 to 7 minutes. Turn oven down to SLOW and keep fritters warm until ready to serve.
4 For the dipping sauce, whisk together the ginger, garlic, vinegar and sesame oil in a small bowl. Float the carrot rounds on top.
5 Arrange the fritters on a platter and serve them with the ginger-garlic dip.

a small saucepan. Boil the juice over medium heat until only 3 tablespoons remain and set it aside.
3 Put the beef into a large bowl and sprinkle it with the lemon rind, cornflour and sugar. Mix well to coat the beef and set the beef aside.
4 Add one third of the beef to the hot pan or wok, distributing it in a single layer. Brown the beef well – it should take 3 to 4 minutes to cook – stirring it frequently. With a slotted spoon, remove the cooked beef. Add 1/2 tablespoon of the oil to the pan or wok and repeat the process with another third of the beef. Remove the second batch. Heat the remaining 1/2 tablespoon of oil and cook the rest of the meat.
5 Once the third batch is well browned, return the already-cooked beef and the rind-and-ginger mixture to the pan or wok. Sprinkle the meat with the salt and the cayenne pepper, then pour in the vinegar and the reduced orange juice. Cook the meat rapidly, stirring often, until all of the liquid has evaporated – approximately 2 minutes.
6 While the beef is cooking, pour enough water into a saucepan to cover the bottom by 2 1/2 cm (1 inch). Set a vegetable steamer in the water, bring the water to the boil, and add the mange-tout. Cover the pan tightly and steam for 2 minutes.
7 Transfer the mange-tout to a warmed serving platter and mound the beef on top. Serve immediately.

Orange-Fried Beef

750 g (1 1/2 lb) sirloin steak, trimmed of fat and sliced into very thin strips
2 oranges
1 tablespoon grated lemon rind
3 tablespoons cornflour
2 tablespoons sugar
2 tablespoons safflower oil
2 teaspoons julienned fresh ginger root
1/4 teaspoon salt
1/8 teaspoon cayenne pepper
4 tablespoons rice vinegar or distilled white vinegar
500g (1 lb) mange-tout, stems and strings removed

1 Carefully pare the rind from the oranges with a sharp knife, leaving the white pith behind. Slice the rind into fine julienne and reserve it.
2 Squeeze the juice from the oranges and pour it into

Broccoli-Studded Prawns/Rice

24 Mediterranean prawns (about 600 g/1¼ lb),
   peeled, tails left on
24 broccoli florets, each stem trimmed to 2½ cm
   (1 inch) long and tapered to a point, blanched for
   1 minute
2 spring onions, trimmed and chopped
1 garlic clove, finely chopped
2 teaspoons finely chopped fresh ginger root
2 tablespoons rice vinegar
2 tablespoons rice wine or dry sherry
1 teaspoon chili paste with garlic
1 teaspoon tomato paste
1 teaspoon cornflour, mixed with 1 tablespoon water
2 tablespoons safflower oil

1 Using a skewer, make a 5 mm (¼ inch) diameter
   hole through each prawn from front to back, about
   one third of the way from its larger end. Insert a
   broccoli stem into the hole so that the floret nestles
   within the curve of the prawn, as shown. Transfer
   the prawns to a bowl with the spring onions, garlic
   and ginger; toss the mixture gently and let it stand
   for at least 10 minutes.
2 While the prawns are marinating, combine the
   vinegar, rice wine or sherry, chili paste, tomato
   paste and the cornflour mixture in a small bowl.
   Set aside.
3 Heat the oil in a wok or heavy frying pan over
   medium-high heat. Add half the prawns and
   gently stir-fry them until they are opaque and firm
   – about 2 minutes. Remove and keep warm. Stir-
   fry the second batch. Return the first batch to the
   wok and pour in the sauce. Stirring gently to coat
   the prawns, cook until the sauce thickens – about
   1 minute. Keep warm in a SLOW oven until ready
   to serve. Serve with boiled rice.

Broccoli-studded prawns/rice.

Added touch

Orange Slices with Pomegranate Seeds

3 oranges
1½ tablespoons finely chopped crystallized ginger
125 ml (4 fl oz) fresh orange juice
1 tablespoon dark rum
2 tablespoons sugar
½ teaspoon pure vanilla extract
4 tablespoons fresh pomegranate seeds

1 Using a sharp stainless steel knife, cut off both
   ends of each orange. Stand the oranges on end
   and cut away vertical strips of the peel and pith.
   Slice the oranges into 5 mm (¼ inch) thick
   rounds.
2 Sprinkle the ginger into the bottom of a 22 cm (9
   inch) pie plate. Arrange the orange slices in a
   spiral pattern, overlapping them slightly, and set
   the pie plate aside.
3 Combine the orange juice, rum and sugar in a
   small saucepan over medium-high heat and boil
   for 5 minutes. Remove the pan from the heat and
   let the syrup cool slightly, then stir in the vanilla
   extract. Pour over the orange slices and chill the
   fruit thoroughly.
4 Invert a serving plate over the pie plate, quickly
   turn both over together, and lift away the pie
   plate. Sprinkle the orange slices with the
   pomegranate seeds, and serve at once.

Shanghai Scallop Soup with 20 Garlic Cloves
Loin and Liver in Yellow Bean Sauce
Parcels of Spring Vegetables with Lemon Butter

What to drink

The combination of scallops, garlic and lamb would suggest a relatively full bodied white Burgundy style.

Start-to-Finish Steps

1 Prepare and assemble the ingredients for each recipe.
2 Follow spring vegetable parcels recipe step 1.
3 Follow step 1 of scallop soup recipe and loin and liver recipe steps 1 and 2.
4 Follow vegetable parcels recipe steps 2 to 5.
5 Follow soup recipe step 2 and spring vegetable parcels recipe step 6.
6 Follow loin and liver recipe steps 3 and 4.
7 Follow soup recipe steps 3 and 4, loin and liver recipe step 5 and vegetable parcels recipe step 7.

Shanghai Scallop Soup with 20 Garlic Cloves

500 g (1 lb) scallops, bright white connective tissue
    removed, larger scallops halved or quartered
2 tablespoons dry sherry
1 tablespoon low-sodium soy sauce or shoyu
Freshly ground black pepper
1½ ltrs (2½ pts) unsalted chicken stock
20 garlic cloves, peeled
250 g (8 oz) bok choy, leaves cut into chiffonade,
    stems sliced diagonally into 5 mm (¼ inch) pieces
4 tablespoons fresh lemon juice
60 g (2 oz) cellophane noodles, soaked in hot water
    for 20 minutes, drained and cut into 2½ cm
    (1 inch) lengths
1 tablespoon chopped fresh coriander

1 Rinse the scallops under cold water and drain. Put them into a bowl with the sherry, soy sauce and some pepper. Gently stir the scallops to coat them with the marinade; set aside.
2 Pour the stock into a large pan and bring it to the boil. Add the garlic cloves, reduce the heat and simmer until the cloves are tender – about 15 minutes.
3 Stir in the bok choy and simmer for 5 minutes more. Stir in the lemon juice, noodles and scallops with the marinade. Cook until the scallops are opaque – about 1 minute.
4 Just before serving, stir in the coriander.

Shanghai scallop soup with 20 garlic cloves. If bok choy (also called Chinese chard) is not available, Swiss chard can be substituted.

Loin and Liver in Yellow Bean Sauce

175 g (6 oz) lean lamb (from the loin), trimmed of fat
    and cut into thin strips
175 g (6 oz) lambs' liver, cut into thin strips
2 teaspoons light low-sodium soy sauce
2 teaspoons Chinese rice wine or dry sherry
1 teaspoon sesame oil
1½ teaspoons cornflour
200 g (7 oz) spring onions
2 cm (¾ inch) piece fresh ginger root
1 garlic clove
2 teapoons safflower oil
½ fresh red chili pepper, seeded and thinly sliced
Nori seaweed, shredded, for garnish

Yellow Bean Sauce

3 tablespoons yellow bean sauce
½ teaspoon sugar
1 teaspoon dark low-sodium soy sauce or shoyu
2 teaspoons Chinese rice wine or dry sherry

Loin and liver in yellow bean sauce.
Suggested accompaniment: egg noodles.

1   Put the loin and liver strips into separate bowls. Blend together the light soy sauce, rice wine, sesame oil and cornflour and divide this marinade between the two bowls. Stir well to coat the meat thoroughly. Leave to marinate for 15 minutes. Mix together the ingredients for the yellow bean sauce and set the sauce aside.

2   Cut the spring onions into 6 cm (2½ inch) lengths. Cut the white sections in half lengthwise; keep the white and green parts separate. Bruise the ginger and garlic with the side of a heavy knife.

3   Heat a wok over medium heat and add the safflower oil. Drop in the ginger and garlic and let them sizzle until they turn light brown. Using the tip of a spatula, rub the garlic and ginger all round the wok, then remove and discard them.

4   Increase the heat to high. Stir-fry the loin, followed by the liver, the white parts of the spring onions and the yellow bean sauce, by constantly tossing and stirring each ingredient for about 15 seconds before adding the next. If the food seems about to stick and burn, lift the wok off the heat for a few seconds. Add the chili and stir-fry for another 10 seconds, then stir in the green parts of the spring onions. Remove from heat.

5   Serve the mixture, garnished with a little shredded nori.

Parcels of Spring Vegetables with Lemon Butter

16 small young carrots about 9 cm (3½ inches) long, scraped, with about 4 cm (1½ inches) of green tops retained
150 g (5 oz) mange-tout, topped and tailed, strings removed
20 thin asparagus spears, trimmed
12 spring onions, trimmed and cut into 10 cm (4 inch) lengths
½ sweet yellow pepper, seeded, deribbed and cut into thin strips
4 teaspoons thinly cut chives
4 teaspoons chopped fresh chervil
4 teaspoons chopped fresh tarragon

Lemon Butter
30 g (1 oz) unsalted butter, softened
1 teaspoon grated lemon rind
1 teaspoon fresh lemon juice
⅛ teaspoon salt
Freshly ground black pepper

1 In a small bowl, mix together all the ingredients for the lemon butter, cover the bowl with plastic film and place it in the refrigerator to chill. Preheat the oven to 220°C (425°F or Mark 7).
2 Pour enough water into a saucepan to fill it about 2½ cm (1 inch) deep. Put a steamer in the pan and bring the water to a boil. Add the carrots, cover them tightly and steam them until they are partially cooked, but still firm – about 8 minutes. Drain them in a colander and transfer them to a large bowl. Toss in the mange-tout, asparagus, spring onions and pepper.

3 Cut out four circles about 25 cm (10 inches) in diameter from parchment paper. Fold each circle in half, crease the parchment, then open it out. Brush each circle lightly with the oil.
4 Spoon a quarter of the vegetables on to a paper circle, keeping the filling to one side of the crease and forming a neat rectangle lying parallel to the fold. Dot the vegetables with a little lemon butter, sprinkle them with 1 teaspoon of each of the herbs and fold over the other half of the paper to enclose the filling.
5 Crimp the edges of the paper, in overlapping double folds, until the package is sealed. Fill and seal the remaining three parcels in the same way.
6 Brush the outside of the packages with a little oil, to prevent the paper from becoming soggy in the oven. Place the parcels on a baking sheet and bake them in the oven for 12 minutes.
7 Serve the sealed packets on individual plates and let the diners pierce and cut open their own parcels to savour the aroma.

Added touch

Spring Onion and Rice Muffins

45 g (1½ oz) long-grain rice
225 g (7½ oz) plain flour
2 teaspoons baking powder
2 teaspoons caster sugar
¼ teaspoon salt
¼ teaspoon ground white pepper
1 egg
175 ml (6 fl oz) semi-skimmed milk
2 tablespoons safflower oil
2 spring onions, trimmed and finely chopped

1 Preheat the oven to 220°C (425°F or Mark 7). Lightly oil a muffin or deep bun tin. Bring 150 ml (¼ pint) of water to the boil in a saucepan. Stir in the rice, then reduce the heat to low, and cover tightly. Cook the rice until it is tender and all the liquid has been absorbed – 15 to 20 minutes. Uncover and set aside to cool.
2 Sift the flour, baking powder, sugar, salt and pepper into a bowl. In another bowl, lightly beat the egg, then whisk in the milk and oil; stir in the cooled rice and the spring onions. Pour the rice mixture into the flour mixture, then stir until the ingredients are just blended.
3 Spoon the batter into the cups in the tin, filling each no more than two-thirds full. Bake the muffins until lightly browned – 18 to 22 minutes. Remove the muffins from the cups immediately and serve hot.

Karen Lee

Menu 1
(*Right*)
Chili Shrimp
Smoked Bean Sprouts
Diced Chicken
with Fermented Black Beans
Rice

Karen Lee, a New York-based author and cooking teacher, describes Chinese cooking as 'physically demanding – an action cuisine,' which is actually both relaxing and fascinating when you know how to approach it. She emphasizes the importance of proper equipment – a sharp knife or cleaver and a good pan – because these make the work go quickly and produce the best results. For a successful stir-fry, she prefers a flat-bottomed wok or heavy skillet. Remember that the essence of stir-frying is speed, so prepare and organize all ingredients in the correct cooking order. Reheat oil between batches and quickly add the ingredients. The food cooks almost at once if the heat is high enough and if you do not overcrowd the pan.

Karen Lee was once the assistant of Grace Zia Chu, a famous Chinese cook, but she has developed her own cooking methods, which stress using little fat or salt. Her recipes are her own versions of Chinese classics and are based on homemade stocks and sauces and the freshest ingredients.

The three menus represent a mélange of Chinese regional fare, with contrasting tastes and colours. In Menu 1, the smokey taste of the bean sprouts offsets the fiery chili shrimp. The orange chicken in Menu 2 is spicy, aromatic, and sweet. Menu 3 features a Northern Chinese favourite, barbecued lamb, served with braised turnips, which Eastern Chinese believe to have a medicinal effect, and Szechwan-style green beans flavoured with dried shrimp and preserved vegetables.

This meal of shrimp, diced chicken, and bean sprouts comes to the table on serving dishes decorated with a delicate Chinese motif. Set off shrimp by turning them out on a bed of lettuce leaves. Chopsticks and straw place mats will add attractive Oriental accents to this simple but authentic menu.

Menu 1

Chili Shrimp
Smoked Bean Sprouts
Diced Chicken with Fermented Black Beans

This chili shrimp dish is typical of Szechwan. Chinese chilies range from the firebrands used in sauces and oils to the larger, milder ones. Chinese cooks often use chilies stirred into a paste with garlic, as in this recipe.

The Chinese frequently cook shrimp with the shells still on, actually scorching the shells to intensify the shrimp flavour. This method has another benefit – it cuts down preparation time.

The smoked bean sprouts and diced chicken breasts are Cantonese. The fermented black beans in the chicken recipe are very pungent, so before using them you may wish to rinse them to remove some of the saltiness.

When buying bean sprouts, avoid the kind that are sold soaking in water. They will not scorch and thus will not take on the proper smokey flavour.

What to drink
Here you need a full-bodied, dry wine: a Burgundy from Mâcon or an inexpensive California Chardonnay.

Start-to-Finish Steps
1 Follow general rice recipe on page 9, step 1. Bring 250 ml (8 fl oz) water to a boil and follow bean sprouts recipe step 1.
2 Follow general rice recipe step 2.
3 Combine marinade ingredients in chicken recipe step 1 and follow steps 2 and 3. Preheat oven to SLOW.
4 Follow bean sprouts recipe steps 2 and 3.
5 Follow shrimp recipe steps 1 and 2.

6 Remove saucepan from heat in rice recipe step 3.
7 Follow bean sprouts recipe steps 4 to 6.
8 Follow chicken recipe steps 4 and 5.
9 Complete bean sprouts recipe steps 7 to 9 and keep warm in preheated oven, if desired.
10 Wipe out wok. Complete chicken, steps 6 to 11.
11 Wipe out wok (or skillet used for bean sprouts). Follow shrimp recipe steps 3 to 6; follow general rice recipe step 4.
12 Remove bean sprouts and chicken from oven. Serve together with shrimp and rice on the side.

Chili Shrimp

The seasoning sauce:
2 tablespoons dry sherry
1 level tablespoon sugar
1 teaspoon Chinese red rice vinegar or Western red wine vinegar
1 tablespoon dark soy sauce
1½ teaspoons light soy sauce
2 tablespoons Chinese Chicken Stock
1 teaspoon water chestnut powder or cornstarch

16 large shrimp (about 500 g (1 lb))
2½ tablespoons plus 2 teaspoons peanut oil
2 whole scallions, chopped
2 teaspoons minced fresh ginger
1 clove garlic, minced
1 teaspoon sesame oil

1 Combine seasoning sauce ingredients in small bowl. Stir to dissolve water chestnut powder or cornstarch.
2 Using small pair of scissors, cut shell along back of shrimp, cutting into shrimp about halfway through. Do not remove shell. Remove dark vein with nose of scissors and pull off legs. Rinse shrimp under cold running water, drain in colander, and pat dry.
3 Heat wok or heavy skillet over high heat about 1 minute. Add 2½ tablespoons peanut oil and heat until hot but not smoking. Add shrimp and stir-fry about 5 minutes, or until shrimp are almost cooked through. Shrimp will be charred and deep orange in colour. Empty shrimp onto warm serving platter.
4 Return pan to high heat and add remaining 2 teaspoons peanut oil. Stir-fry scallions, ginger, and garlic 30 seconds.

5   Stir seasoning sauce once more and add it all at once to wok or skillet, stirring until sauce thickens slightly.
6   Return shrimp to pan and stir another minute, or until shrimp are evenly coated with sauce. Turn off heat and swirl in sesame oil. Empty contents onto serving platter.

Smoked Bean Sprouts

4 Chinese dried black mushrooms
1 medium-size leek, white part only
350 g (12 oz) mung bean sprouts
1 teaspoon water chestnut powder or cornstarch
1 tablespoon oyster sauce
1 1/2 teaspoons dark soy sauce
1 tablespoon dry sherry
1 1/2 tablespoons peanut oil

1   Cover mushrooms with 250 ml (8 fl oz) boiling water and allow to soak 20 to 30 minutes.
2   Cut off root end of leek. Slice leek in half lengthwise and rinse under warm water to remove all sand. Cut into 7 1/2 cm (3 inch) lengths; then shred. Set aside in small bowl.
3   Place sprouts on layers of paper towels and pat dry.
4   Squeeze each mushroom over bowl. Using strainer lined with double thickness of cheesecloth or paper towels, strain and reserve 1 tablespoon of the liquid. Remove tough stems, rinse under cold water to get rid of any grit trapped in gills, and shred mushrooms. Add to leeks.
5   Combine water chestnut powder or cornstarch, oyster sauce, soy sauce, and sherry with the tablespoon of mushroom soaking liquid. Stir to dissolve.
6   Heat wok or skillet over high heat 2 minutes. Add bean sprouts, reserving a sprinkling for garnish, if desired. Stir-fry without oil 2 or 3 minutes, or until sprouts begin to scorch. Transfer cooked sprouts to flat serving dish.
7   Return wok or skillet to high heat and add peanut oil. Immediately add mushrooms and leeks, and stir-fry 2 minutes.
8   Stir oyster sauce mixture once more and add to the vegetables all at once, stirring until sauce thickens.
9   Add the cooked bean sprouts and mix briefly. Empty contents onto serving dish. This dish may be eaten hot or served at room temperature, garnished with a sprinkling of some fresh sprouts, if desired.

Diced Chicken with Fermented Black Beans

1 egg white
1 tablespoon water chestnut powder or cornstarch
1 tablespoon dry sherry
500 g (1 lb) skinless chicken breasts

The seasoning sauce:
3 tablespoons dry sherry
1 tablespoon dark soy sauce
1 1/2 teaspoons light soy sauce
1/2 teaspoon sugar
1 teaspoon water chestnut powder or cornstarch
100g (3 oz) shallots (about 10 whole)
2 teaspoons minced fresh ginger
1 clove garlic, minced
1 1/2 tablespoons fermented black beans
750 ml (1 1/2 pts) peanut oil

1   Combine egg white, water chestnut powder or cornstarch, and dry sherry in medium-size bowl and stir vigorously about 1 minute, or until marinade is smooth.
2   Remove any cartilage and fat from chicken. Cut into bite-size pieces and add to marinade, tossing well until chicken is evenly coated.
3   Combine seasoning sauce ingredients in small bowl. Stir to dissolve water chestnut powder or cornstarch.
4   Peel shallots and leave them whole.
5   Combine ginger, garlic, and black beans in small bowl.
6   Heat wok over high heat about 1 minute. Pour in peanut oil and heat until oil reaches 180°c (350°F) or until a sliver of garlic sizzles on contact.
7   Stir chicken in marinade. Turn heat to high and add mixture to pan all at once, stirring in circular motion about 1 1/2 minutes, or until chicken turns opaque.
8   Turn off heat and carefully drain chicken and hot oil in metal colander set over large bowl.
9   Return 1 tablespoon of the oil to the wok or to a heavy skillet and add shallots. Stir occasionally over low heat about 3 minutes, or until shallots are cooked through.
10 Turn heat to high and add ginger, garlic, and black beans. Stir another minute.
11 Stir seasoning sauce and add it to the pan along with the cooked chicken. Stir another minute, or until chicken is evenly coated. Empty pan onto heated serving dish and keep warm in oven.

<table>
<tr><td>

Menu

2
</td><td>

Orange Chicken
Stir-Fried Sugar Snap Peas
Stir-Fried Spinach with Fermented Bean Curd
</td></tr>
</table>

Red peppers, scallion tops, and orange peel create an appetizing mélange of colour with browned chicken thighs. The peas and stir-fried spinach add two more contrasting greens. Garnish the meal with semi-circles of orange.

28

The crisp chicken dish in this menu is an excellent example of Szechwan cooking, successfully combining the sting of chilies in the chili paste with the mild aftertaste of the slightly sweet seasoning sauce. Orange peel, a favourite Szechwan flavouring, is also an ingredient. If you cannot find dried Chinese orange or tangerine peel, substitute fresh grated peel. Just be sure to grate the peel only; do not include any of the bitter white pith.

The sugar snap peas are likely to scorch, so stir-fry them quickly over medium heat. Snow peas work equally well, and can be cooked the same way. If you must store them for a few days, wrap the unwashed peas in a plastic bag and refrigerate.

Both the chicken and the spinach recipes call for water chestnut powder as a thickening agent. Cornstarch is less expensive and perfectly adequate – and also more readily available – but use the chestnut powder if possible; it is lighter and gives a more luminous cast to foods. To remove any lumpiness, pulverize the powder in a blender and store it in an airtight jar. You will find water chestnut powder in Chinese groceries.

The fermented bean curd in the stir-fried spinach recipe has a strong, cheesy taste when mashed. Available in Chinese groceries as bottled cubes, it keeps indefinitely in the refrigerator. Several brands are seasoned with chili flakes. Buy one of these if you like extra spice. There are no Western equivalents. If you cannot find fermented bean curd, simply omit bean curd from the recipe; plain bean curd is not a substitiute.

What to drink
Here, a medley of delicate flavours calls for an equally delicate wine with a light touch of sweetness. A German wine – say a Riesling Kabinett or, possibly, an Auslese (which is slightly sweeter than Kabinett) should be your first choice. Look for one from the Rheingau or the Rheinhessen.

Start-to-Finish Steps
1 Follow chicken recipe steps 1 and 2.
2 Follow spinach recipe steps 1 and 2, and snow peas recipe step 1.
3 Grate fresh orange or tangerine peel, if using, and follow chicken recipe steps 3 to 6.
4 Slice scallions in spinach recipe, step 3.
5 Complete chicken recipe, steps 7 to 16.
6 Wipe out wok. Complete spinach recipe steps 4 to 6. If you desire warm spinach, keep in oven with chicken while you finish preparing snow peas.

7 Wipe out wok or skillet for spinach. Follow snow peas recipe steps 2 and 3. Serve platter of chicken with snow peas and pass the spinach separately.

Orange Chicken

The chicken and marinade:
1 kg (2 lb) chicken thighs
1 egg white
1 level tablespoon plus 2 teaspoons water chestnut powder or cornstarch
1 tablespoon dry sherry

The seasoning sauce:
1 teaspoon water chestnut powder or cornstarch
3 tablespoons dry sherry
1 tablespoon dark soy sauce
1 tablespoon light soy sauce
2 tablespoons Chinese chicken stock
2 level tablespoons sugar
1 teaspoon chili paste
1 teaspoon Chinese red rice vinegar
1 medium-size red bell pepper
3 whole scallions
3 pieces Chinese dried orange or tangerine peel, approximately 3½ by 5 cm (1½ by 2 inches), or 1 teaspoon grated fresh peel
750 ml (1½ pts) peanut oil
2 teaspoons minced fresh garlic
2 cloves garlic, minced
2 teaspoons sesame oil
1 orange, halved and sliced for garnish (optional)

1 Remove skin from chicken thighs and cut away any fat. Using heavy cleaver or chef's knife, cut chicken thighs crosswise through bone into 3½ cm (1½ inch) pieces.
2 Combine marinade ingredients in large bowl and add chicken pieces. Stir vigorously about 1 minute, until marinade is smooth and chicken is evenly coated. Cover and refrigerate until ready to cook.
3 Combine seasoning sauce ingredients in small bowl. Stir to dissolve water chestnut powder or cornstarch.
4 Core and seed red pepper and split in half. Slice into 1 cm (½ inch) squares. Cut each square into 2 triangles.
5 Firmly grasp scallions together and slice them into 5 mm (¼ inch) rounds. Break orange peel into 5 mm (¼ inch) pieces.
6 Heat wok over high heat about 1 minute. Pour in 750 ml (1½ pts) peanut oil and turn heat to medium. Heat oil until it reaches 180°C (350°F) on deep-fat thermometer.
7 Stir chicken once more in marinade. Raise heat to

high and add half the chicken pieces and marinade to the oil, stirring occasionally to prevent chicken pieces from sticking together. Cook about 3 to 5 minutes, or until chicken is lightly browned.

8   Using Chinese mesh or long-handled slotted metal spoon, remove chicken pieces from oil and place them on baking sheet lined with several layers of papertowels. before frying remaining chicken, bring oil back to temperature.

9   To finish cooking chicken (this gives it a crispy crust), heat oil to 190°C (375°F). Return one quarter of the chicken to the oil and fry 1 minute, or until chicken is well browned. Drain on fresh paper towels and fry remaining chicken in batches.

10 Pour off all but 1 tablespoon of the hot oil.

11 Preheat oven to SLOW.

12 Turn heat to low, add scallions, ginger, and garlic, and stir-fry 15 seconds.

13 Add dried or fresh grated peel and stir-fry until it turns a darker brown, about 1 minute.

14 Raise heat to high, add red pepper, and stir-fry 30 seconds.

15 Stir seasoning sauce and add it to pan all at once, stirring until sauce thickens slightly, about 15 seconds.

16 Return cooked chicken to pan all at once and stir-fry rapidly until chicken has been evenly glazed with the sauce. Turn off heat and add sesame oil, stirring to blend. Empty contents onto heated flat serving dish and keep warm in oven. Garnish serving dish or plates with orange slices, if desired. *Note:* If desired, oil may be heated to 190°c (375°F) in step 6 and chicken fried 5 to 6 minutes, or until golden brown. This would eliminate the second frying process in step 9.

Stir-Fried Sugar Snap Peas

350 g (12 oz) sugar snap peas or snow peas
2 tablespoons peanut oil
1/2 teaspoon salt
1/2 teaspoon sugar

1   String peas and rinse under cold running water. drain and dry well with paper towels or in salad spinner.

2   Heat wok or skillet over high heat about 1 minute. Add peanut oil and heat until hot but not smoking. Lower heat to medium and add salt and sugar, stirring a few seconds.

3   Add sugar snaps or snow peas and stir-fry continuously 1 minute. Remove peas and arrange them around chicken on serving platter like spokes of a wheel, if you wish.

Stir-Fried Spinach with Fermented Bean Curd

The seasoning sauce:
1 teaspoon water chestnut powder or cornstarch
1 tablespoon dry sherry
1 small square fermented bean curd, mashed (optional)
1/2 teaspoon sugar

750 g (1 1/2 lb) fresh spinach
White distilled vinegar
2 whole scallions
1 tablespoon peanut oil
1/2 teaspoon salt
1 clove garlic, minced
1 teaspoon sesame oil

1   Combine seasoning sauce ingredients in small bowl. Stir to dissolve water chestnut powder or cornstarch.

2   Remove stems from spinach and wash in several changes of cold water to which several dashes of white vinegar have been added – it helps rid spinach of any grit.. Dry with paper towels or in salad spinner.

3   Firmly grasp scallions together and slice them into 1 cm (1/2 inch) rounds.

4   Heat wok or heavy skillet over high heat about 1 minute. Add peanut oil and heat until it is hot but not smoking. If a piece of scallion sizzles when added, oil is hot enough. Add salt and stir until it dissolves. Add garlic and scallions, and stir-fry 30 seconds.

5   Add spinach and stir-fry about 2 minutes, or until leaves wilt.

6   Stir seasoning sauce and add it to pan all at once, stirring until spinach is evenly coated with sauce. Turn off heat and add sesame oil, stirring to mix. Empty contents onto serving dish. The spinach may be served warm or at room temperature.

<table>
<tr>
<td>

Menu

3
</td>
<td>

Barbecued Lamb
Sautéed Green Beans, Szechwan Style
Braised Turnips with Black Mushrooms
</td>
</tr>
</table>

Precision-cut turnips and trimmed green beans add visual appeal to this menu of barbecued lamb cubes. Muted in colour, the meal benefits from a sprinkling of sliced scallion greens, which complements the green beans.

The barbecued lamb marinated in black tea and fragrant with garlic and hot chili oil is a Northern Chinese dish that is particularly good grilled on an outdoor barbecue in summer. Various cuts of beef, such as sirloin, flank, or shell steak, or fillet mignon, make good substitutes for lamb. Instead of a Chinese sesame paste for the lamb's marinade, Karen Lee uses tahini, a Middle Eastern condiment, whose flavour she prefers for this recipe.

Green beans that are deep-fried and then quickly stir-fried are a famous Szechwan dish. Despite their double cooking, the beans retain their natural crispness. The cooks of this far Western region often add ground pork to the beans for extra protein and flavour. In this version dried shrimp and Tientsin preserved vegetable also flavour the beans. The tiny dried shrimp have a salty taste and a strong odour, and are valued as a highly seasoned condiment. There is no comparable Western substitute. The preserved vegetable is shredded cabbage, which adds a distinctive crunch and saltiness to the recipe. It is sold in bulk in plastic bags, or in ceramic crocks in Chinese shops.

The turnips are easy to do. You steam them briefly, then stir-fry, and finally braise them in a rich liquid. You can make them ahead if you wish and quickly reheat them, taking care not to overcook them. Their soft texture is an interesting contrast to the crunchy beans.

What to drink

The interplay of sweet and spicy flavours in this meal makes choosing a wine a challenge. You might serve beer or, even better, a good ale. For a wine, try a French Colombard or perhaps a Semillon. Their softness will accomodate the variety of tastes in the menu.

Start-to-Finish Steps

In the morning: Bring 175 ml (6 fl oz) water to a boil and follow lamb recipe steps 1 to 4.

1   Bring 500 ml (1 pt) water to a boil. Use half for shrimp in green beans recipe step 1 and the other half for mushrooms in turnips recipe step 1.
2   Remove lamb from refrigerator and bring to room temperature, step 5. If using bamboo skewers, soak in water to prevent scorching.
3   Follow turnip recipe steps 2 and 3.
4   Follow lamb recipe step 6.
5   Follow green beans recipe steps 2 and 3.
6   Follow lamb recipe step 7 and turnip recipe steps 4 and 5.
7   If using double oven, preheat oven to SLOW. If using single-oven, turn off heat. Follow lamb recipe step 8.
8   Complete turnip recipe steps 6 and 7, and keep warm in oven.
9   Wipe out wok. Follow green beans recipe steps 4 to 9.
10 Remove barbecued lamb and cooked turnips and mushrooms from oven. Serve with green beans.

Barbecued Lamb

1 level tablespoon black tea leaves
125 g (4 oz) tahini (sesame seed paste)
3 tablespoons dark soy sauce
1½ tablespoons sesame oil
1 tablespoon hot chili oil
1½ level tablespoons sugar
1½ tablespoons Wetern red wine vinegar
2 whole scallions, chopped
2 cloves garlic, minced
750 g (1½ lb) boneless leg of lamb

1   Pour 175 ml (6 fl oz) boiling water over tea leaves in large bowl and steep 5 minutes. Strain 125 ml (4 fl oz) tea into cup. Discard leaves.
2   Return tea to large bowl and combine with remaining ingredients except lamb, and stir to mix well.
3   Using Chinese cleaver or chef's knife, cut lamb into bite-size cubes.
4   Add lamb to marinade. Turn lamb to coat well and seal tightly. Refrigerate.
5   Thirty minutes before cooking, remove lamb from refrigerator.

6 Preheat grill.
7 Place 4 or 5 cubes of lamb on each skewer, leaving 1 cm ($^1/_2$ inch) between cubes. Place skewers $2^1/_2$ cm (1 inch) apart on grill rack and set rack as close as possible to heat source.
8 Grill 8 to 10 minutes, turning frequently. keep warm in oven.

Sautéed Green Beans, Szechwan Style

1 teaspoon dried shrimp
500 g (1 lb) gren beans
1 tablespoon dark soy sauce
1 tablespoon dry sherry
1 teaspoon chili paste
1 teaspoon honey
750 ml (1$^1/_2$ pts) peanut oil
125 g (4 oz) minced pork
2 teaspoons minced fresh ginger
1 level tablespoon Tientsin preserved vegetable
1 whole scallion, chopped

1 In small bowl, cover shrimp with boiling water and allow to soak 20 minutes. Drain and mince.
2 Cut off stem ends of green beans, leaving pointed ends intact. Wash beans and dry them well so they will not spatter when frying.
3 Combine soy sauce, sherry, chili paste, and honey in small bowl.
4 Heat wok over high heat about 1 minute. Pour in oil and heat over medium heat until oil reaches 190°C (375°F) on deep-fat thermometer. Or test, test oil with a green bean: it should sizzle and the oil foam around it.
5 Turn heat to high and carefully add green beans all at once. Deep-fat fry them until they wrinkle, about 3 minutes. Drain beans and hot oil in colander set over large bowl. Alternatively, you may use a Chinese mesh spoon or long-handled slotted metal spoon and quickly scoop out beans and drain them in a metal colander.
6 Return 1 tablespoon of the hot peanut oil to the wok or to a heavy skillet and turn heat to high. Add minced pork and stir about 2 minutes, or until pork turns white.
7 Add shrimp, ginger, preserved vegetable, and scallions. Cook, stirring, another minute.
8 Stir soy sauce mixture to recombine ingredients and add it to pan all at once, stirring a few seconds.
9 Add cooked, drained green beans and stir-fry another minute, or until sauce is completely absorbed. Empty contents of pan onto heated flat serving dish and serve immediately.

Braised Turnips with Black Mushrooms

5 to 6 Chinese dried black mushrooms
500 g (1 lb) small white turnips
1 level tablespoon sugar
1 tablespoon dark soy sauce
1 tablespoon dry sherry
1$^1/_2$ tablespoons peanut oil

1 Cover mushrooms with 250 ml (8 fl oz) boiling water and allow to soak 20 to 30 minutes.
2 Peel turnips and cut into $2^1/_2$ cm (1 inch) cubes.
3 Bring $2^1/_2$ cm (1 inch) water to a boil in large saucepan fitted with a vegetable steamer. Steam turnips 10 minutes.
4 Squeeze each mushroom over small bowl in which mushrooms soaked. Strain and reserve 125 ml (4 fl oz) of the liquid. Remove tough stems and rinse mushrooms under cold running water to rid of any grit trapped in gills. Cut each mushroom into quarters or eighths, depending on its size.
5 Add sugar, soy sauce, and sherry to bowl with reserved mushroom liquid.
6 Heat wok or heavy skillet over high heat about 1 minute. Add peanut oil and heat until hot but not smoking. Add mushrooms and turnips, and stir-fry about 1 minute.
7 Stir soy sauce mixture before adding it to pan. Stir until turnips and mushrooms are evenly glazed. Turn into heated serving dish.

Leftover suggestion
The marinade for the lamb also makes a very good dip for lightly blanched or raw vegetables. Bring it to a boil before serving. The barbecued lamb is particularly good served the next day. Bring it to room temperature. Do not reheat it; the meat will dry out. the leftover green beans, if, any, combined with greens, make an excellent salad.

Added touch
Ripe, fresh fruit, served with scented or semi-fermented tea, brings any Chinese meal to a satisfying close. Pineapple and strawberries, when they are in the market, are a good combination. Slice off the top and bottom of a fresh pineapple, and save the top. Cut the body into 6 sections lengthwise. Remove the hard inner core and separate the fruit from the rind with your knife. Then cut each piece into 6 sections vertically. Place the top of the pineapple in the centre of a serving platter and arrange the 6 sections around it, so that they radiate outward like wheel spokes. Scatter whole strawberries around the spokes and sprinkle with 125 ml (4 fl oz) Grand Marnier.

John Bentley

Menu 1
(*Left*)
Four-Season Dumplings with Sweet-and-Sour-Sauce
Stir-Fried Vegetables with Shredded Lamb
Eight-Treasure Noodles with Chinese Sausage

John Bentley had hardly thought about a career in the restaurant business when he first began cooking with a wok.

'I had absolutely no interest in cookery at the time, but I was a student living on a very low income with a two-ring gas stove. Wok cooking suited my meagre income, and my cooking facilities and abilities. I just flung everything together and hoped for the best.'

Now the owner of a flourishing restaurant on the West coast, his attitudes towards cookery have certainly changed, but his fondness for the wok has remained.

'It's a healthy way to cook, as well as being quick and convenient,' he affirms. He has visited China several times and greatly admires the variety of regional Chinese cuisines and the ingenuity of the Chinese.

'Nothing is wasted, if it's fresh, they will find a way to cook it. They also have a wealth of tradition in preserving food, whether by drying or pickling.' John's menus reflect his wide knowledge of Chinese-style cookery and are geared to suit a wide range of tastes. Menu 3 is totally meatless, but is substantial enough to suit vegetarian and carnivore alike. The colours, textures and flavours of each dish have been carefully chosen to delight both the eye and the palate.

Four-Season Dumplings make a colourful start to the meal.
Present them in the bamboo steamer, allowing the guests to serve themselves.

Menu

1

Four-Season Dumplings with Sweet-and-Sour Sauce
Stir-Fried Vegetables with Shredded Lamb
Eight-Treasure Noodles with Chinese Sausage

What to drink

The strong flavours in this menu require perhaps a fuller bodied Australian Chardonnay or Semillon/Chardonnay.

Start-to-Finish Steps

1 Prepare and assemble the ingredients for each recipe.
2 Prepare dipping sauce for dumplings and set aside.
3 Follow vegetables and lamb recipe step 1 and noodles recipe step 1.
4 Follow dumplings recipe steps 2 and 3.
5 Follow vegetables and lamb recipe steps 2 and 3. Wipe out wok.
6 Follow noodles recipe steps 2 and 3.
7 Follow dumplings recipe step 4 and noodles recipe step 4.

Four-Season Dumplings with Sweet-and-Sour Sauce

175 g (6 oz) gyoza wrappers, or wonton wrappers cut into circles
175 g (6 oz) lean pork, trimmed of all fat and finely chopped
60 g (2 oz) cooked prawns, peeled and finely chopped
1 tablespoon dry sherry
2 tablespoons grated fresh ginger root
1 garlic clove, very finely chopped
3 spring onions, trimmed and very finely chopped
60 g (2 oz) sweet potato or carrot, grated
2 teaspoons low-sodium soy sauce or shoyu
$1/2$ teaspoon fresh lemon juice
2 teaspoons very finely chopped fresh coriander
4 tablespoons diced water chestnuts
2 dried shiitake or Chinese black mushrooms, soaked in very hot water for 20 minutes, stems removed, cut into 5 mm ($1/4$ inch) squares
$1/8$ sweet red pepper, seeded, deribbed and cut into 5 mm ($1/4$ inch) squares
2 tablespoons shelled peas

Sweet-and Sour-Sauce
3 tablespoons frozen orange juice

4 tablespoons unsalted chicken stock
2 tablespoons fresh lemon juice
2 tablespoons rice vinegar
1 tablespoon oyster sauce
1 tablespoon sugar
1 tablespoon unsalted tomato paste
2 teaspoons cornflour

1 Combine the sauce ingredients in a small pan and stir them together until the cornflour is dissolved. Bring the sauce to the boil, stirring constantly until it thickens. Set the pan aside.
2 To make the filling, combine the pork, prawns, sherry, ginger, garlic, spring onions, sweet potato or carrot, soy sauce, lemon juice, coriander and 3 tablespoons of the water chestnuts in a large bowl. Place a scant teaspoon of the filling in the centre of a gyoza or wonton wrapper and form it into a dumpling. Garnish each of the four openings with one piece each of mushroom, red pepper, pea and the remaining water chestnuts.
3 Using a paper towel or a pastry brush, lightly oil the floor of a steamer. Arrange as many of the dumplings inside as will fit without touching. Cover the steamer, set it in a pot filled with $2 1/2$ cm (1 inch) of boiling water, and steam the dumplings over high heat for 8 minutes. Remove the dumplings and set them aside on a tray or serving platter; cover them with aluminium foil and put them in a low oven to keep them warm. Cook the remaining dumplings the same way, oiling the steamer floor before adding each new batch.
4 Meanwhile re-warm the dipping sauce over low heat, stirring occasionally. Serve the dumplings hot; pass the dipping sauce separately.

Stir-Fried Vegetables with Shredded Lamb

350 g (12 oz) lean lamb (from the loin), cut into thin strips
4 tablespoons sake or dry sherry
2 tablespoons low-sodium soy sauce or Shoyu
1 teaspoon cornflour
2 tablespoons safflower oil
1 tablespoon finely chopped fresh ginger root
1 onion, peeled and sliced
175 g (6 oz) baby sweetcorn, halved lengthwise if large
1 sweet red pepper, seeded, deribbed and thinly sliced
175 g (6 oz) small mange-tout, stems and strings removed

1 Mix together the sake, soy sauce and cornflour in a small bowl and set the mixture aside.
2 Heat the oil in a wok or large, heavy sauté pan until it is hot but not smoking. Add the chopped ginger and onion slices, and stir-fry for 1 minute over high heat, then add the baby sweetcorn and continue to stir-fry for 1 more minute.
3 Lastly, add the mange-tout and stir-fry for 1 minute. Pour the sake mixture over the meat and vegetables in the wok and bring it to the boil, stirring until the liquid thickens. Keep warm in a SLOW oven until ready to serve.

Eight-Treasure Noodles with Chinese Sausage

250 g (8 oz) dried flat wheat noodles or fettuccine
1 ltr (1 3/4 pts) unsalted chicken stock
1 1/2 tablespoons safflower oil
1 tablespoon grated fresh ginger root
1 small red onion, cut into 2 cm (3/4 inch) squares
3 lop cheong sausages, thinly sliced diagonally, simmered for 5 minutes in water to cover and drained, or 125 g (4 oz) barbecue pork, cut into 3 mm (1/8 inch) slices
175 g (6 oz) mange-tout, trimmed and halved diagonally
8 shiitake or Chinese black mushrooms, soaked in very hot water for 20 minutes, drained, stemmed and quartered
450 g (15 oz) canned baby sweetcorn, drained, rinsed
450 g (15 oz) canned straw mushrooms, drained
125 g (4 oz) broccoli florets, blanched in boiling water for 1 minute, refreshed under cold water and drained
2 teaspoons cornflour, mixed with 2 tablespoons water
1 tablespoon low-sodium soy sauce or shoyu
1 tablespoon rice vinegar
1 tablespoon dark sesame oil

1 Reduce the stock to about 1/4 ltr (8 fl oz) and keep it hot.
2 Add the noodles to 4 litres (7 pts) of boiling water with 2 teaspoons of salt; start testing them after 3 minutes and cook them until they are *al dente*. Drain the noodles and rinse them with cold water.
3 In a hot wok, heat the oil over medium-high heat. When the oil is hot but not smoking, add the ginger and onion, and stir-fry them for 30 seconds Put in the red pepper, sausage, mange-tout, shiitake or Chinese black mushrooms and baby sweetcorn, and continue stir-frying for 1 minute. Add the straw mushrooms, broccoli and cauliflower, and stir-fry until all ingredients are very hot – about 1 minute more.
4 Stir the cornflour mixture, soy sauce and vinegar into the hot stock. Pour this sauce into the wok and stir until it thickens, adding the sesame oil at the last minute. Put the noodles in the wok, toss them with the vegetables to heat them through, and then serve the dish immediately.

<table>
<tr><td>

Menu

2

</td><td>

Nest of the Phoenix
Spring Vegetable Stir-Fry
South-East Asian Beef Noodles

</td></tr>
</table>

What to drink

Because of the predominance of vegetable a very light white wine such as an Orvieto or Frascati would be suitable.

Start-to-Finish Steps

1   Assemble and prepare ingredients for each recipe. Follow Nest of the Phoenix step 1 and beef noodles recipe step 1.
2   Follow Nest of the Phoenix recipe steps 2 to 6.
3   Follow beef noodles recipe steps 2 to 4.
4   Assemble Nest of the Phoenix — steps 7 and 8.
5   Clean out wok and prepare vegetable stir-fry, steps 1 and 2.
6   Follow beef noodles recipe step 5. Serve.

Nest of the Phoenix

500 g (1 lb) flat rice noodles
600 g (1¼ lb) cooked peeled prawns
125 ml (4 fl oz) fresh lime juice
1 teaspoon grated lime rind
3 teaspoons sweet chili sauce
4 tablespoons chopped fresh mint
1 tablespoon chopped fresh coriander
250 g (8 oz) mange-tout, stems and strings removed, blanched in boiling water for 1 minute, drained and julienned
2 teaspoons low-sodium soy sauce or shoyu
½ teaspoon dark sesame oil
1 tablespoon chopped fresh basil
1½ tablespoons safflower oil
2 teaspoons finely chopped fresh ginger root
3 large carrots, peeled and julienned
6 tablespoons fresh lemon juice
5 spring onions, sliced diagonally into very thin ovals
300 g (10 oz) fresh bean sprouts, rinsed and drained
3 tablespoons unsweetened coconut milk
½ tsp salt
1½ teaspoons finely chopped fresh citrus leaf, centre vein removed, or 1½ teaspoons grated lime rind

Garnish

1 round lettuce
1 large sweet red pepper, seeded, deribbed and halved lengthwise, each half sliced crosswise into thin strips
Mint sprigs
2 lemons (optional), each cut into 8 wedges

1   In large bowl, combine the prawns, 2 tablespoons of the lime juice, the lime rind, 1 teaspoon of the sweet chili sauce, 1 tablespoon of the chopped mint and the tablespoon of chopped coriander. Set the bowl aside.
2   In another bowl, combine the mange-tout with the soy sauce, sesame oil and basil. Set that bowl aside too.
3   Pour enough boiling water over the noodles to cover them, and let them soak for 15 minutes. drain the noodles and rinse them in cold water; drain them again thoroughly and set them aside.
4   While the noodles are soaking, pour ½ tablespoon of the safflower oil into a heated wok or a heavy frying pan over high heat. When the oil is hot, add the ginger and the carrots. Reduce the heat to medium and stir-fry the carrots for 1 minute. Add 2 tablespoons of water, cover the wok, and steam the contents for 2 minutes. Transfer the steamed carrots to a bowl and toss them with 2 tablespoons of the lemon juice. Set the bowl aside.
5   Wipe out the wok and heat the remaining tablespoon of safflower oil in it. Add the spring onions and stir-fry them for 30 seconds, then add the bean sprouts and stir-fry them for 1 minute more. Spread the spring onions and sprouts on a plate so they may cool.
6   Prepare the dressing for the noodles: in a large bowl, combine the coconut milk, salt and citrus leaf or rind with the remaining 6 tablespoons of lime juice, the 2 teaspoons of sweet chili sauce, the remaining 3 tablespoons of mint and the remaining 4 tablespoons of lemon juice. Toss the dressing with the drained noodles and set them aside.
7   To assemble the nest of the Phoenix, line a very large platter with the lettuce leaves. Fill the dish with the noodles, making a wide, shallow well in their centre. Tuck the red pepper strips betwen the lettuce leaves and the noodles all the way round the dish.
8   Arrange the carrots in a ring about 5 cm (2 inches) in from the edge of the noodles. Next make a smaller circle of the mange-tout just inside the carrot ring, then a ring of the onion and sprout mixture just inside the mange-tout. Mound the prawns in the centre and garnish the phoenix nest with the mint sprigs and the lemon wedges if you are using them. Serve at room temperature.

38

Spring Vegetable Stir-Fry

2 tablespoons virgin olive oil
30 g (1 oz) pine-nuts (optional)
30 g (1 oz) fresh ginger root, peeled and finely chopped
2 garlic cloves, crushed
125 g (4 oz) French beans, topped and tailed
125 g (4 oz) mange-tout, topped and tailed
125 g (4 oz) broccoli florets (optional)
125 g (4 oz) asparagus, trimmed, stems finely sliced diagonally
125 g (4 oz) carrots, peeled and thinly sliced diagonally
1/2 each small sweet red, green and yellow peppers, seeded and finely sliced
3 sticks celery, thinly sliced
3 spring onions, trimmed, thinly sliced diagonally
1/4 teaspoon salt

1   Heat 1 teaspoon of the oil in a large frying pan. Add the pine-nuts and fry gently until they turn golden-brown. Remove them from the pan and set them aside.
2   Pour 1 tablespoon of oil into the pan and heat. Add the ginger and garlic and cook for 2 to 3 seconds, then add the beans and stir-fry for about 2 minutes. Add the mange-tout, stir-fry for about 1 minute, then add the broccoli, asparagus and carrots, and stir-fry for 2 minutes more. Add the remaining oil, the peppers, celery, and spring onions, and stir-fry until the vegetables are just tender – 2 to 3 minutes. Season with the salt, and stir in the reserve pine-nuts.
3   Transfer to a hot serving dish and garnish, if liked, with finely sliced spring onions. Serve immediately.

South-East Asian Beef Noodles

600 g (1 1/4 lb) rump steak, trimmed of fat and cut into paper-thin slices
1 tablespoon low-sodium soy sauce or shoyu
2 tablespoons dry sherry or dry white wine
2 tablespoons sugar
Freshly ground black pepper
1 1/2 tablespoons cornflour
175 g (6 oz) Asian wheat noodles, or 125 g (4 oz) vermicelli
4 teaspoons safflower oil
1 small onion, halved and sliced lengthwise
1 carrot, peeled, halved lengthwise and thinly sliced on the diagonal
250 g (8 oz) broccoli stems, peeled, halved lengthwise and thinly sliced on the diagonal
1/2 sweet red pepper, seeded, deribbed and cut into narrow strips about 5 cm (2 inches) long
2 teaspoons finely chopped fresh ginger root
4 garlic cloves, finely chopped.
1/4 ltr (8 fl oz) unsalted brown or chicken stock
1/2 tablespoon sweet chili sauce, or 1/2 teaspoon hot red pepper flakes mixed with 1/2 teaspoon golden syrup and 1/2 teaspoon rice vinegar
1 tablespoon fresh lemon juice
1 tablespoon hoisin sauce or low-sodium soy sauce

1   In a large bowl, combine the beef slices with the tablespoon of soy sauce, the sherry or white wine, 1 tablespoon of the sugar, some pepper and 1/2 tablespoon of the cornflour. Set the mixture aside.
2   Put the noodles into 3 ltrs (5 pts) of boiling water. Start testing the noodles or vermicelli after 3 to 5 minutes and cook them until they are *al dente*. Drain the pasta in a colander and rinse it under very hot water. Drain the pasta again and transfer it to a serving platter. Cover the platter with foil to keep the pasta warm.
3   Heat 2 teaspoons of the oil in a large, non-stick frying pan or well-seasoned wok over high heat. Add the onion slices and stir-fry them for 1 minute. Add the carrot and broccoli, and stir-fry them for 1 minute. Mix in the sweet red pepper and stir-fry the mixture for 2 minutes more. Mound the vegetables on top of the pasta, then cover the platter with the foil once more, and keep it warm.
4   Heat the remaining 2 teaspoons of oil in the pan or wok over high heat. Add the ginger and garlic, and stir-fry them until the ginger is light brown — about 2 minutes. Add the beef along with its marinade, and stir-fry it until no traces of pink remain — 1 to 2 minutes. Spoon the beef mixture on to the centre of the vegetables and keep the platter warm.
5   Pour the stock into a pan and bring it to the boil. While the stock is heating, mix the remaining cornflour with 2 tablespoons of water in a small bowl. Stir into the stock the cornflour mixture, chili sauce or red-pepper-flake mixture, the remaining sugar, the lemon juice, and the hoisin sauce or soy sauce. Reduce the heat and simmer the mixture until it thickens — about 1 minute. Pour the sauce over the beef and serve it immediately.

<table>
<tr><td>

</td><td>

Tofu with Sweet Pepper and Peanuts, Szechwan-Style
Stir-Fried Vegetables in a Sweet-and-Sour Sauce
Stir-Fried Chinese Cabbage and Plantain

</td></tr>
</table>

What to drink

This fully vegetarian menu with spicy flavours would be best suited by a slightly spiced or peppered Gewürztraminer.

Start-to-Finish Steps

1 Follow tofu recipe steps 1 and 2. Assemble and prepare all the ingredients for each recipe.
2 Follow vegetables in sweet-and-sour sauce recipe step 1.
3 Follow tofu recipe steps 3 to 5. Wipe out wok.
4 Follow vegetables in sweet-and-sour sauce recipe steps 2 to 4, transfer to a warm serving dish and wipe out wok.
5 Prepare cabbage and plantain. Serve.

Tofu with Sweet Pepper and Peanuts, Szechwan-Style

2 tablespoons safflower oil
1 kg (2 lb) firm tofu, well drained, cut into 2 cm (3/4 inch) cubes
2 garlic cloves, thinly sliced
4 cm (1 1/2 inch) piece fresh ginger root, peeled and finely shredded
3 fresh or dried red chili peppers, seeded and thinly sliced
8 spring onions, green and white parts separated and thinly sliced
2 small sweet green peppers, seeded, deribbed and cut into 1 1/2 cm (3/4 inch) squares
1/8 teaspoon salt
1 tablespoon rice wine or sherry
45 g (1 1/2 oz) shelled peanuts, skinned and toasted

Seasoning Sauce

2 tablespoons low-sodium soy sauce or shoyu
2 teaspoons rice wine or vinegar
1 1/2 teaspoons sugar
100 ml (3 1/2 fl oz) unsalted vegetable stock or water
1 1/2 teaspoons cornflour
1/2 teaspoon Tabasco or chili sauce

1 In a non-stick frying pan, heat 2 teaspoons of the oil and fry half of the tofu cubes over medium-high heat for 3 to 5 minutes, until they are golden-brown all over; turn the cubes continuously with a spatula to prevent the tofu from sticking to the pan. Transfer the cubes to paper towels to drain. Pour another 2 teaspoons of the oil into the pan, fry the remaining tofu cubes in the same way, and transfer them to paper towels.
2 In a small bowl, mix together all the ingredients for the sauce. Set the sauce aside.
3 Heat the remaining oil in a wok or large, heavy frying pan, swirling it round to coat the sides. Drop in the garlic and allow it to sizzle for a few seconds. Add the ginger and fry, stirring continuously, until it is golden-brown – about 2 minutes. Add the chilies and the white parts of the spring onions, and stir-fry for 10 seconds, turning and tossing the ingredients with a spatula. Add the sweet peppers, stir-fry for 10 seconds, then add the tofu cubes and stir-fry for a further 20 seconds. Add the salt and wine.
5 Stir the sauce well and pour it into the wok. Continue to stir over the heat until the sauce thickens; add the peanuts. Remove the wok from the heat and mix in most of the green parts of the spring onions. Transfer the tofu stir-fry to a serving dish and sprinkle over the remaining spring onions. Keep warm until ready to serve.

Stir-Fried Vegetables in a Sweet-and-Sour Sauce

1 1/2 tablespoons safflower oil
350 g (12 oz) baby sweetcorn, trimmed if necessary, halved lengthwise
1 large sweet red pepper, seeded, deribbed and cut into strips
350 g (12 oz) young carrots, trimmed and thinly sliced diagonally
350 g (12 oz) bean sprouts
350 g (12 oz) mange-tout, strings removed
2 teaspoons dark sesame oil
Fresh gound black pepper

Sweet-and-Sour-Sauce

3 teaspoons arrowroot
300 ml (1/2 pt) unsweetened pineapple juice
2 tablespoons low-sodium soy sauce or shoyu

1 tablespoon freshly grated ginger root
1 garlic clove, crushed
150 ml (¼ pt) unsalted vegetable stock
1 teaspoon clear honey
5 spring onions, trimmed and finely sliced

1 To make the sweet-and-sour sauce, place the arrowroot in a medium-sized saucepan and gradually blend in the pineapple juice. Stir in the soy sauce or shoyu, grated ginger, garlic, vegetable stock, honey and sliced spring onions. Bring the contents of the pan to the boil, reduce the heat, and simmer the sauce for 5 minutes, stirring it frequently. Set the sauce aside while you cook the vegetables.
2 Heat the safflower oil in a wok or large, heavy frying pan over high heat. ad the sweetcorn, red pepper and carrots, and stir-fry them for 4 minutes. Add the bean sprouts and mange-tout, and stir-fry for a further 1 to 2 minutes, until the vegetables are cooked but still slightly crunchy.
3 Add the sweet-and-sour sauce to the wok. Reduce the heat and cook the mixture for 1 to 2 minutes more, still stirring, to warm the sauce through.

4 Season the stir-fry with the sesame oil and with some freshly ground black pepper. Serve.

Stir-Fried Chinese Cabbage and Plantain

1 kg (2 lb) Chinese cabbage, shredded
1 tablespoon safflower oil
4 spring onions, sliced diagonally into 1 cm (½ inch) pieces
1 ripe plantain, sliced into thin rounds
½ teaspoon crushed red pepper flakes
3 tablespoons rice vinegar or cider vinegar

1 In a wok or a large, heavy-bottomed frying pan, heat the oil over high heat. Add the spring onion and plantain pieces and stir-fry for 1 minute. Add the cabbage and red pepper flakes; cook, stirring constantly, until the cabbage wilts – 1 to 2 minutes more. Pour in the vinegar and cook for 1 minute. Transfer the cabbage and plantain to a large dish and serve immediately.

Stir-fried vegetables in a sweet-and-sour sauce. Serve with brown rice.

42

Mai Leung

Menu 1
(*Left*)
Spinach and Egg Shred Soup
Diced Chicken, Szechwan Style
Stir-Fried Green Beans
with Garlic Rice

Cooking teacher and author Mai Leung is another cook who believes that Chinese cuisine is effortless – once you learn the basic methods. She advises her beginning students to follow recipes carefully until they gain confidence but then to experiment with ingredients and seasonings. She also stresses the importance of understanding the differences in spices and sauces. For instance, there are several kinds of soy sauce and oyster sauce, varying in aroma and flavour. As you use them, you will learn to recognize the most subtle distinctions and to know when to use one rather then another in a particular recipe.

When she was living in Hong Kong, Mai Leung learned to cook in the southern style of that area. She studied with chefs from other regions as well and gained even more knowledge of other regional approaches during her travels throughout China.

In Canton and Hong Kong, southern coastal regions that are famous for their abundant fresh oysters, residents rarely eat oysters raw, but they have created innumerable oyster-based recipes. Oyster fritters are featured in Menu 2, and oyster sauce (made from ground oysters) flavours the beef and scallop dish in Menu 3.

Oriental dinnerware and bamboo place mats set off the brilliant colours of this Szechwan meal of diced chicken and stir-fried green beans. A glass soup bowl shows off the clarity of the broth, which is filled with crisp spinach and slivers of white egg 'pancake.'

**Spinach and Egg Shred Soup
Diced Chicken, Szechwan Style
Stir-Fried Green Beans with Garlic/Rice**

This spicy meal of diced chicken, garlicky stir-fried green beans, and a clear broth contains no ingredients unfamiliar to Westerners. The soup is a typical Chinese broth embellished with crisp vegetables and slivers of cooked egg, meant to be refreshing rather than filling. You may serve the soup as an appetizer or with the main course.

The Szechwan-style stir-fried chicken dish is made zesty by the use of dried red chilies. Serving stir-fried green beans with cooked ground pork, as in this recipe, is a typical Szechwan way of combining tastes and textures.

What to drink

This Szechwan-style menu, with its marked presence of hot peppers and garlic, will go well with a lightly sweet wine: try a German Riesling from the Rheingau.

Start-to-Finish Steps

1   Follow diced chicken recipe step 1.
2   Follow spinach soup recipe step 1.
3   Follow general rice recipe on page 9, steps 1 and 2.
4   Peel and mince ginger; slice scallions; rinse and quarter water chestnuts; seed, trim, and chop red bell pepper. Follow chicken recipe steps 2 to 4.
5   Follow spinach soup recipe steps 2 to 4.
6   Follow general rice recipe step 3.
7   Follow diced chicken recipe steps 5 to 8.
8   Preheat oven to SLOW. Follow stir-fried green beans recipe steps 1 to 4.
9   Complete diced chicken recipe, steps 9 to 12.
10 Wipe out pan. Follow stir-fried green beans recipe steps 5 to 7.
11 Follow spinach soup recipe step 5 and general rice recipe step 4. Serve.

Spinach and Egg Shred Soup

125 g (4 oz) fresh spinach
1 ltr (1³/₄ pts) Chinese Chicken stock
1 egg, lightly beaten with ¹/₄ teaspoon salt
1 tablespoon peanut or corn oil
¹/₄ teaspoon sugar
¹/₂ teaspoon sesame oil
Salt to taste

1   Wash spinach well, rinsing to remove any grit or sand. Snap off any tough stems. Drain in colander.
2   Bring chicken stock to a boil in large saucepan. Reduce to a simmer and cover.
3   Heat small skillet over moderate heat and add cooking oil, turning pan to film bottom. When oil is hot, swirl in egg mixture to make large thin pancake. When egg is set – it will take only a minute – flip egg and turn off heat.
4   Transfer 'pancake' to chopping board and cut into thin strips. Set aside.
5   Turn spinach into the simmering stock and turn off heat. Stir in sugar, sesame oil, and egg strips. Add salt to taste. Serve hot.

Diced Chicken, Szechwan Style

1 tablespoon dried cloud ear mushrooms
500 g (1 lb) skinless, boneless chicken breasts (about 2 whole breasts)
1 egg white, lightly beaten
1 level tablespoon plus 2 teaspoons cornstarch
2 level tablespoons sugar
1 tablespoon dark soy sauce
1 tablespoon white vinegar
2 tablespoons Chinese rice wine or dry sherry
1¹/₂ tablespoons ketchup
1 tablespoon water
¹/₈ teaspoon Cayene pepper
¹/₄ teaspoon salt
2 teaspoons sesame oil
2 dried red chili peppers
2 thin slices fresh ginger, peeled and minced
3 scallions, cut into thin rounds
6 water chestnuts, thoroughly rinsed and quartered

½ small red bell pepper, seeds and ribs removed, cut into 1 cm (½ inch)
500 g (1 pt) peanut or corn oil
30 g (1 oz) raw unsalted peanuts, shelled and hulled

1 Cover dried cloud ears with 250 ml (8 fl oz) hot water and allow to soak 20 minutes, or until they are soft and triple in size.
2 Pound chicken breasts gently with flat side of cleaver or with meat pounder. Trim any fat and cut into 1 cm (½ inch) cubes. Put lightly beaten egg white in large mixing bowl and slowly stir in 1 level tablespoon cornstarch, to combine well. Add cubed chicken and toss well. Set aside.
3 Combine sugar, remaining cornstarch, soy sauce, vinegar, wine, ketchup, water, Cayene pepper, salt, and sesame oil in small bowl.
4 Group chili peppers, minced ginger, scallions, water chestnuts, and red bell pepper on tray or large plate.
5 Drain and tear each cloud ear into 4 or 5 pieces. Set aside.
6 Heat wok over high heat until a bead of water evaporates on contact. Add cooking oil and heat until very hot but not smoking – a good test is to see whether a small piece of scallion sizzles when dropped in the oil. Add peanuts and turn heat to medium-low. Deep-fry peanuts until golden brown, about 3 to 5 minutes. Remove with Chinese mesh spoon or long-handled slotted metal spoon and put on paper towels to drain.
7 Add chicken mixture to the hot oil and turn off heat. Separate chicken pieces with wooden spoons. As soon as chicken pieces turn white, use Chinese mesh spoon or slotted metal spoon to remove them to a plate lined with paper towels and set aside.
8 Pour off all but 2 tablespoons of warm cooking oil into a container. (Strain and save cooking oil for other Chinese dishes.)
9 Return wok to high heat or use a large, deep skillet to which you have added 2 tablespoons of warm cooking oil. When oil is very hot, add chili peppers, which are used to flavour the oil, and cook until they turn dark red. Remove and discard.
10 Add ginger, half the scallions, the cloud ears, water chestnuts, and red bell pepper. Stir-fry 3 or 4 seconds.
11 Stir soy sauce mixture, swirl it into the vegetables, and cook, stirring until sauce begins to bubble. Return chicken to pan and cook, stirring constantly, for several seconds to reheat. Transfer to serving platter and top with peanuts and remaining scallions.
12 Keep warm in preheated SLOW oven while preparing other dishes.

Stir-Fried Green Beans with Garlic

500 g (1 lb) fresh young green beans, washed and trimmed
¼ teaspoon salt
½ teaspoon sugar
1 tablespoon dark soy sauce
1 tablespoon Chinese rice wine or dry sherry
2 tablespoons Chinese rice wine or dry sherry
2 tablespoons water
2 scallions
2 tablespoons peanut or corn oil
3 medium-size cloves garlic, minced
60 g (2 oz) ground pork

1 Bring 2½ ltrs (4 pts) water to a boil in a large saucepan.
2 Add green beans and blanch about 45 seconds over moderate heat, then pour into colander and rinse under cold running water to stop the cooking. Drain.
3 Combine salt, sugar, soy sauce, wine, and water in small bowl.
4 Wash and trim scallions, leaving some of green tips, and slice them in half lengthwise. Cut into 3½ cm (1½ inches) thick.
5 Heat wok or heavy skillet over high heat until a bead of water evaporates on contact and add oil. When oil is hot, add scallions and garlic, and stir fry 4 or 5 seconds. Add ground pork and stir-fry continuously until it loses its pink colour, about 1 to 2 minutes.
6 Stir soy sauce mixture and swirl into wok. Add green beans and stir over moderate heat about 1 minute, or just until they are heated through.
7 Cover and keep warm until ready to serve.

Five-Fragrance Oyster Fritters
Steamed Sesame Aubergine
Jade-Green Broccoli

Crisp vegetables set off this light meal, where the emphasis is on steaming and blanching rather than on stir-frying. Both broccoli and aubergine must be very fresh.

Cantonese chefs have created numerous delicious oyster-based recipes. These fritters, seasoned with Chinese five-spice, white pepper, and sliced scallions, are served with a ginger-soy-vinegar dipping sauce.

What to drink
The oysters need a crisp, lightly sweet wine, such as a California Semillon or Chenin Blanc.

Start-to-Finish Steps
1 Shuck oysters, if using fresh ones, and follow oyster fritter recipe steps 1 to 3.
2 Peel aubergine and follow recipe step 1.
3 Follow broccoli recipe steps 1 to 3.
4 Follow aubergine recipe steps 2 to 4.
5 Preheat oven to SLOW. Follow oyster fritter recipe steps 4 to 6.
6 Follow aubergine recipe steps 5 to 7.
7 To finish, follow broccoli recipe step 5, aubergine recipe step 8, and oyster fritter recipe step 7. Serve.

Five-Fragrance Oyster Fritters

Ginger-Soy-Vinegar Dip:
2 thin slices ginger, peeled and finely chopped
2 tablespoons dark soy sauce
60 ml (2 fl oz) Chinese red rice vinegar
16 to 18 large fresh oysters, shucked, or two 250 g (8 oz) containers shucked oysters, drained
4 eggs
2 tablespoons plus 125 ml (4 fl oz) peanut or corn oil
100 g (3 oz) plain flour
1½ teaspoons baking powder
1½ teaspoons Chinese five-spice
1 teaspoon salt
¼ teaspoon freshly ground white pepper
3 scallions, white and some green, cut into thin rounds
1 head lettuce for garnish (optional)

1 Bring 1 ltr (1¾ pts) water to a rolling boil in large saucepan.
2 Combine ingredients for dip in small serving bowl.

This light meal of oyster fritters, aubergines, and broccoli is served attractively on an interestingly shaped dinner plate nested in a bamboo tray. Accompany the fritters with a bowl of the dipping sauce.

3 Add oysters to the boiling water and remove from heat. Pour oysters into strainer and immerse in bowl of cold water. Drain and pat dry with paper towels. Set aside.

4 In large mixing bowl, beat eggs with 2 tablespoons of the peanut or corn oil until foamy. Add dry ingredients. Beat until smooth. Stir in scallions and oysters.

5 Heat heavy skillet over moderate heat and add two thirds of the remaining oil. When oil is hot but not smoking, spoon 2 to 3 tablespoons of batter with 1 or 2 oysters into the skillet: there should be room for 3 to 4 fritters.

6 Cook, turning them, until both sides are golden brown. Keep warm in oven while you finish cooking remaining oyster-batter mixture. Add more oil as needed.

7 Serve hot on a bed of lettuce, if desired, with ginger-soy-vinegar dip.

Steamed Sesame Aubergine

1 Aubergine, (500 g (1 lb) peeled
1 level tablespoon raw sesame seeds
3 tablespoons *hoisin* sauce
1 tablespoon dark soy sauce
1 teaspoon Chinese rice wine or dry sherry
3 scallions
2 tablespoons peanut or corn oil
1 teaspoon sesame oil

1 Cut aubergine into strips 10 cm (4 inches) long and 1 cm ($^1/_2$ inch) wide.

2 Bring $2^1/_2$ cm (1 inch) of water to a boil in medium-size saucepan for steaming. Place aubergine on vegetable steamer, cover, and steam over medium-high heat for 3 to 5 minutes, or until aubergine is soft. Turn off heat and leave cover on.

3 Heat small saucepan over moderate heat. Add sesame seeds and stir constantly with wooden spoon. When they turn golden brown, remove from heat and transfer to small plate to cool. Wipe out pan.

4 Combine *hoisin* sauce, soy sauce, and wine or sherry in small bowl. Set aside.

5 Trim scallions, leaving some of the green tops, and cut into $3^1/_2$ cm ($1^1/_2$ inch) lengths. Shred each piece lengthwise.

6 Heat peanut or corn oil in the small saucepan. When oil is hot, add two thirds of the shredded scallions. Stir and cook several seconds, or until scallions soften.

7 Add hoisin mixture and stir over medium to high heat. When sauce bubbles, turn off heat. Add sesame oil.

8 Remove aubergine to serving bowl and pour sauce over. Top with toasted sesame seeds and remaining scallion.

Jade-Green Broccoli

4 tablespoons peanut or corn oil
1 small bunch broccoli
2 tablespoons oyster sauce
1 tablespoon dark soy sauce
1 teaspoon sesame oil
1 tablespoon Chinese rice wine or dry sherry

1 Bring $2^1/_2$ ltrs (4 pts) water to a boil in large saucepan for blanching broccoli. Add 2 tablespoons of the peanut or corn oil.

2 Wash broccoli and discard tough leaves. Cut florets into finger-length pieces. Peel tough stems and cut stems diagonally into thin slices. Set aside.

3 Combine remaining peanut or corn oil, oyster sauce, soy sauce, sesame oil, and wine or sherry in small saucepan. Set aside.

4 Blanch broccoli in the boiling water 1 minute, then remove with Chinese mesh spoon or slotted metal spoon. Shake off excess water and place on serving platter.

5 Heat oyster sauce mixture over moderate heat. When sauce begins to bubble, remove from heat and pour over broccoli.

**Pork Shreds and Szechwan Pickle Soup
Beef and Scallops with Oyster Sauce
Stir-Fried Snow Peas with Mushrooms and
Almonds/Rice**

Varied in colour, flavour, and texture, the beef with scallops, stir-fried snow peas with miniature ears of corn, and shredded pork and pickle soup make a pleasing display against bamboo or wood.

48

The Chinese do not eat as much beef as Westerners do and do not raise beef cattle. Instead, their beef comes from water buffalo or oxen, long past their prime, so that the meat is tough and strong-tasting. Cantonese chefs rarely serve anything resembling a steak but shred the meat to make it more palatable, then tossing it together with a variety of other ingredients, such as the scallops and oyster sauce in this recipe.

The Szechwan pickle in the soup is not at all like the Western-style preserved cucumber. Instead, it is a hot, spiced preserved mustard green root with a unique flavour. There are no Western substitutes, but the pickle is readily sold in Chinese markets, either loose in a crock or in cans.

What to drink

Try a full-bodied, dry white wine with the full flavours here: an inexpensive California Chardonnay or, even better, a fully dry Sauvignon Blanc; a white Burgundy from Mâcon or an inexpensive Chablis; an Italian Greco di Tufo or a fully dry Orvieto.

Start-to-Finish Steps

1 Prepare Szechwan pickle for soup, step 1.
2 Follow general rice recipe on page 9, steps 1 and 2.
3 Follow beef with scallops recipe steps 1 to 5.
4 Follow pork soup step 2.
5 Prepare snow peas, drain and halve water chestnuts, and follow stir-fried snow peas recipe steps 1 to 4.
6 Bring soup stock to a simmer, step 3.
7 Follow beef with scallops recipe steps 6 to 9.
8 Preheat oven to SLOW. Follow pork soup recipe step 4.
9 Complete beef with scallops recipe steps 10 and 11. Follow general rice recipe step 3.
10 Wipe out pan. Cook stir-fried snow peas recipe steps 5 and 6.
11 Follow pork soup recipe step 5. Remove platters of beef with scallops and stir-fried snow peas from oven. Serve with rice.

Pork Shreds and Szechwan Pickle Soup

5 cm (2 inch) chunk Szechwan pickle
125 g (4 oz) lean pork cutlet or boned pork chop
2 teaspoons cornstarch
1 teaspoon light soy sauce
1 teaspoon light sesame oil
1 ltr (1 ¾ pts) unsalted Chinese Chicken Stock
1 scallion

1 Thoroughly wash pickle in warm water to rinse off all spices. Cut it into thin shreds and soak in small bowl with 1 ltr (1¾ pts) water about 20 minutes. Rinse and drain.
2 Cut pork cutlets into thin shreds. In small bowl combine cornstarch, soy sauce, and sesame oil. Add the shredded pork and toss well.
3 In medium-size saucepan, bring chicken stock and soaked pickle to a simmer, and cover.
4 Wash and trim scallion, leaving some of green top. Cut into thin rounds.
5 Add pork mixture to the simmering stock, separating the pieces with a fork. Simmer about 20 seconds, or until pork shreds are no longer pink. Add scallion and salt to taste. Serve hot.

Beef and Scallops with Oyster Sauce

1 tablespoon dark soy sauce
2 teaspoons sesame oil
2 level tablespoons plus 2 teaspoons cornstarch
1 teaspoon sugar
500 g (1 lb) flank steak
60 ml (2 fl oz) oyster sauce
3 tablespoons plus 2 teaspoons Chinese rice wine or dry sherry
2 tablespoons water
4 scallions
1 thin slice fresh ginger, peeled and minced
2 medium-size cloves garlic, minced
1 small red bell pepper, seeds and ribs removed, cut into thin strips
6 ears baby corn, rinsed and cut in half lengthwise
6 water chestnuts, rinsed and cut in half
250 g (8 oz) scallops
500 ml (1 pt) peanut or corn oil

1 Combine soy sauce, sesame oil, 2 tablespoons of the cornstarch, and ¼ teaspoon of the sugar in large mixing bowl and stir well.
2 Using cleaver or knife held at an angle, cut flank steak on the diagonal (against fibre) into thin

pieces 5 cm (2¹/₂ inches) long. Add to soy marinade and toss, making sure to coat all the beef slices. Set aside.

3   In small bowl, combine oyster sauce with remaining ³/₄ teaspoon sugar, Chinese rice wine, and water, and set aside.

4   Wash and trim scallions, leaving some of green tops. Cut in half lengthwise and then into 1 cm (¹/₂ inch) pieces. Place ginger, garlic, pepper, baby corn, and water chestnuts in separate piles on medium-sized plate.

5   If using sea scallops, cut them in half. Leave bay scallops whole. Put scallops in medium-size bowl. Add remaining 2 teaspoons of cornstarch. Toss gently to mix well.

6   Heat wok over high heat and add peanut or corn oil. When oil is very hot but not smoking – a good test is to see whether a small piece of scallion sizzles when dropped in – add beef mixture and gently separate pieces with 2 long-handled wooden spoons. Cook beef over high heat about 1 minute, or until beef just loses its redness. Remove with Chinese mesh spoon or long-handled slotted metal spoon and shake off any excess oil. Turn onto another medium-sized plate lined with paper towels to drain further.

7   Turn heat to low and add scallops. Cook about 30 seconds. Remove scallops with chinese mesh spoon or slotted metal spoon to the plate with the beef.

8   Pour off all but 2 tablespoons of oil from the wok. (You may strain and save the oil for cooking other Chinese dishes.) Turn heat to high and heat oil until it is very hot. Add scallions, ginger, and garlic. When garlic turns golden, about 2 seconds, add red pepper, baby corn, and water chestnuts. Stir about 10 seconds, or until just heated through.

9   Add oyster sauce mixture and stir until it bubbles.

10 Return beef and scallops (along with any juices that have accumulated on plate) to pan. Stir several seconds to reheat.

11 Immediately remove food to heatproof platter. Cover with foil and keep warm in oven.

Stir-Fried Snow Peas with Mushrooms and Almonds

250 g (8 oz) snow peas, washed and strings removed
6 ears baby corn, cut in half lengthwise
60 g (2 oz) Chinese straw mushrooms
6 water chestnuts, drained and halved
1 tablespoon dark soy sauce
1 tablespoon water
2 teaspoons oyster sauce
1 tablespoon Chinese rice wine or pale dry sherry
1 teaspoon sesame oil
¹/₄ teaspoon salt
¹/₄ teaspoon sugar
1 scallion
60 ml (2 fl oz) peanut or corn oil
30 g (1 oz) sliced almonds

1   Bring 1¹/₂ ltrs (3¹/₂ pts) water to a boil in large saucepan.

2   Add snow peas, baby corn, straw mushrooms, and water chestnuts. Immediately pour them into metal colander and rinse under cold water to stop the cooking. Drain and set aside on medium-size plate.

3   In small mixing bowl, combine soy sauce, oyster sauce, water, wine or sherry, sesame oil, sugar, and salt. Stir well and set aside.

4   Trim scallion, leaving some of green top. Cut in half lengthwise and then into 3¹/₂ cm (1¹/₂ inch) pieces. Set aside on small plate.

5   Heat wok or heavy skillet over moderate heat. Add peanut or corn oil. When oil is hot, add almonds and cook, stirring about 30 seconds, until golden brown. Turn off heat and remove almonds with Chinese mesh spoon or slotted metal spoon to drain on paper towels.

6   Pour off all but 2 tablespoons of oil from the pan. Turn heat to high. When oil is hot, add chopped scallion and cook 3 to 4 seconds. Add blanched snow peas, baby corn, straw mushrooms, and water chestnuts. Stir-fry for about 20 seconds. Stir and swirl in oyster sauce mixture. Stir several seconds, then transfer to serving platter. Top with the toasted almonds and keep warm in oven.

Added touch

Fresh fruit is always welcome after a Chinese meal. try this simple orange dessert:

1   Peel 3 chilled oranges and cut crosswise into thin slices.
2   Remove seeds and divide slices into equal portions on serving plates.
3   Sprinkle small amount of sweetened coconut flakes and chopped crystalized ginger on top.
4   Garnish with fresh mint, if available.

Added Touch

Fresh fruit in Ginger Syrup

1 tart green apple, quartered, cored and cut into 1 cm (1/2 inch) pieces
2 ripe peaches or nectarines, halved, stoned and cut into 1 cm (1/2 inch) pieces

1 pear, peeled, cored and cut into 1 cm (1/2 inch) pieces
225 g (7 1/2 oz) blueberries, picked over and stemmed
3 tablespoons fresh lemon juice
2 tablespoons julienned orange rind
5 cm ginger root, cut into 5 mm (1/4 inch) rounds
135 g (4 1/2 oz) sugar

1   Place the apple, peaches, pear and blueberries in a large bowl. Pour the lemon juice over the fruit and toss well, then refrigerate the bowl.
2   Pour 1 ltr (1 3/4 pts) of water into a large, heavy-bottomed saucepan over medium-high heat. Add the orange rind, ginger and sugar, and bring the mixture to the boil. Reduce the heat to medium and simmer the liquid until it is reduced to about 1/2 ltr (16 fl oz) of syrup. Remove the ginger with a slotted spoon and discard it.
2   Pour the syrup into a large bowl and let it stand at room temperature for about 10 minutes. Add the fruit to the syrup and stir gently to coat the fruit. Refrigerate the dessert, covered, until the fruit is thoroughly chilled – about 1 1/2 hours.

Fresh fruit in ginger syrup. If blueberries are not available, bilberries, stoned cherries or seedless grapes may be used.

Francis Morton

Menu 1
(*Left*)
Rice Congee
Warm Szechwan Noodles
with Spiced Beef
Lamb and Broccoli Stir-Fry

Francis Morton inherited his love of Chinese-style cookery. His maternal grandmother was Chinese and passed on her knowledge of Chinese traditions to Francis through his mother. Thus blessed with a background of two strikingly different cultures, Francis used his skills as a cook to combine the best of both Eastern and Western cooking traditions. His menus reflect this. In Menu 1, the Szechwan Noodles with Spiced Beef, hot to the palate, are well-balanced with the milder Lamb and Broccoli Stir-fry. In Menu 2, Chinese noodles are used unusually in a spicy salad, and the Nonya Rice Noodles recipe adds another dimension to his cookery, with Malaysian influences.

Francis appreciates the 'instant' aspect of Wok cookery but stresses that the selection of really fresh ingredients, especially meat and fish, is of paramount importance when preparing food in this way.

Rice Congée
Warm Szechwan Noodles with Spiced Beef
Lamb and Broccoli Stir-Fry

What to drink

With this menu which features beef and lamb it is possible to use a light red wine such as Beaujolais or a pungent rosé such as Côtes du Provence.

Start-to-Finish Steps

1 Assemble and prepare the ingredients for each recipe.
2 Follow rice congée recipe step 1.
3 After reducing the rice to a simmer for rice congée, follow noodles and beef recipe steps 1 to 3, then rice congée recipe step 2.
4 Follow rice congée recipe step 3.
5 Wipe out wok ready for lamb recipe.
6 Follow lamb recipe steps 1 and 2.
7 Serve rice congée, then noodles with beef and lamb and broccoli.

Rice Congée

135 g (4½ oz) long-grain rice
1 ltr (1¾ pts) unsalted brown or chicken stock
1 tablespoon safflower oil
6 garlic cloves, finely chopped
60 g (2 oz) fresh ginger root, julienned
125 g (4 oz) bean sprouts
45 g (1½ oz) Fresh coriander leaves
1 lime, cut into 16 wedges
2 tablespoons sugar
1 teaspoon fish sauce or low-sodium sauce
1 teaspoon salt
Freshly ground black pepper
250 g (8 oz) beef fillet, trimmed of fat and cut into thin strips
3 spring onions, trimmed and cut into 1 cm (½ inch) lengths

1 Put the rice, stock and 1 ltr (1¾ pts) of water into a large saucepan; bring the liquid to the boil. Stir the mixture, then reduce the heat to medium, and simmer the rice, uncovered, until it is very soft and begins to break apart – about 1 hour.
2 While the rice is cooking, heat the safflower oil in a small frying pan over medium-low heat. Add the garlic and cook it, stirring often, until it is crisp and brown – 4 to 5 minutes. Transfer the garlic to a paper towel towel and let it drain. Put the garlic, ginger, bean sprouts, coriander and lime wedges into small serving bowls, and set them aside.
3 About 5 minutes before serving, stir the sugar, fish sauce or soy sauce, salt and some pepper into the hot soup. Add the beef strips and spring onions, and bring the liquid to the boil. Reduce the heat to medium and simmer the soup until the beef is just cooked – about 3 minutes. Keep hot.
4 Ladle the soup into individual bowls. Pass the garnishes separately inviting diners to season their own soup with them.

Warm Szechwan Noodles with Spiced Beef

500 g (1 lb) fresh Chinese egg noodles, or 350 g (12 oz) dried vermicelli
350 g (12 oz) beef fillet or lean sirloin, trimmed of all fat
8 dried shiitake or Chinese black mushrooms, soaked in very hot water for 20 minutes and drained
4 spring onions, thinly sliced diagonally
1/2 tablespoons safflower oil

Sesame-Soy Marinade
4 tablespoons low-sodium soy sauce or shoyu
2 tablespoons Chinese black vinegar or balsamic vinegar
2 tablespoons rice vinegar
1 to 2 tablespoons chili paste with garlic
1/2 tablespoons very finely chopped garlic
1/2 tablespoons very finely chopped fresh ginger root
1 teaspoon sugar
1 teaspoon dark sesame oil
2 tablespoons safflower oil
2 tablespoons toasted sesame seeds, crushed with a mortar and pestle
5 spring onions, very finely chopped
30 g (1 oz) fresh coriander, coarsely chopped

Garnish
1 small cucumber, scored lengthwise with a fork and thinly sliced
1 tablespoon toasted sesame seeds
Coriander sprigs

1 Combine the marinade ingredients in a bowl and set the marinade aside.
2 Cut the beef across the grain into julienne about 4 cm (1 1/2 inches) long and 3 mm (1/8 inch) thick. Cut off and discard the mushroom stems, and slice the caps into strips about 3 mm (1/8 inch) wide. In a bowl, combine the beef, mushrooms and spring onions and one third of the marinade. Let the beef marinate for 30 minutes.
3 At the end of the marinating time, put 4 litres (7 pts) of water on to boil. Drain and discard any excess marinade from the beef mixture. Heat the 1 1/2 tablespoons of safflower oil in a heavy frying pan or wok; add the mushrooms, spring onions and beef strips, and sauté them for 1 minute. Set the beef mixture aside on a large plate, spreading it out so that it cools rapidly.
4 Add the noodles to the boiling water. Start testing them after 3 minutes and cook until *al dente*. Drain the noodles and transfer them to a large bowl. Add the remaining marinade and toss it with the noodles.
5 To serve, arrange the cucumber slices in an overlapping pattern around the edge of a large plate. Arrange the noodles in the centre of the plate, partly covering the cucumber. Make a shallow well in the centre of the noodles and spoon the beef mixture into the well. Sprinkle the sesame seeds over all and garnish with a few coriander sprigs. Serve at room temperature.

Lamb and Broccoli Stir-Fry

350 g (12 oz) lean lamb (from the loin), cut into thin strips
4 teaspoons safflower oil
20 g (3/4 oz) fermented black beans, soaked in water for 5 minutes
1/2 teaspoon sesame oil
1 onion, halved lengthwise, cut into strips
2 garlic cloves, finely chopped
2 1/2 cm (1 inch) piece fresh ginger root, finely chopped
175 g (6 oz) broccoli, blanched, stalks peeled and julienned, flowers divided into florets
2 sticks celery, chopped
1 sweet red pepper, seeded, deribbed and thinly sliced
1 teaspoon low-sodium soy sauce or shoyu
200 g fresh water chestnuts, peeled and boiled for 3 minutes, or canned water chestnuts, drained
3 tablespoons medium sherry

1 Heat 1 teaspoon of the safflower oil in a wok or a large heavy frying pan and stir-fry half of the lamb over a medium heat, tossing and stirring until it is browned – about 2 minutes. remove the lamb from the wok and keep it warm. Heat another teaspoon of the oil in the wok, stir-fry the remaining meat and add it to the first batch.
2 Drain the black beans and mash them in a small bowl with the sesame oil to make a coarse paste. Set aside. Put the remaining safflower oil into the wok or frying pan, add the onion, chopped garlic and ginger and stir-fry for 1 minute. Add the broccoli, celery, red pepper and soy sauce and stir-fry for a further 2 minutes. add the water chestnuts, black bean paste and sherry, and return the lamb to the wok. Stir-fry over medium heat for a further 2 minutes, so that all the ingredients are coated with the sauce and heated through. Keep warm until ready to serve.

Hot and Sweet Soup with Seafood Dumplings
Shining Noodle Salad with Beef and Tomato
Nonya Rice Noodles with Prawns

What to drink

Try some of the new wines coming from South Africa in increasing numbers. A light Chardonnay or a Blanc de Noir would suit this menu.

Start-to-Finish Steps

1 Follow shining noodle salad recipe steps 1 and 2. While the beef marinates, follow soup and dumplings recipe step 1, then shining noodle salad step 3 and Nonya rice noodles recipe step 1.
2 Follow soup and dumplings recipe step 2. Keep soup hot until ready to serve.
3 Follow shining noodle salad recipe step 4.
4 Follow Nonya rice noodles recipe steps 2 to 4. Serve.

Hot and Sweet Soup with Seafood Dumplings

250 g (8 oz) finely chopped lean pork
250 g (8 oz) fresh prawns, peeled. deveined if necessary, and finely chopped
250 g (8 oz) white crab meat, picked over
2 spring onions, trimmed and finely chopped
1^1/$_2$ teaspoons finely chopped fresh ginger root
1 egg white beaten
2 ltrs (3^1/$_2$ pts) unsalted chicken stock
2 teaspoons sweet chili sauce, or 1 teaspoon crushed hot red pepper flakes mixed with 2 teaspoons golden syrup and 1 teaspoon vinegar
125 ml (4 fl oz) fresh lemon juice
250 g (8 oz) small cantaloupe melon balls
^{1}/$_4$ teaspoon salt

1 Combine the pork, prawns, crab meat, spring onions, ginger and egg white in a large bowl. Shape heaped teaspoonfuls of the mixture into dumplings about 2^1/$_2$ cm (1 inch) in diameter, moistening your palms from time to time to keep the mixture from sticking to them.
2 Pour the stock into a large pan and bring it to the boil. Reduce the heat to maintain a strong simmer and add the chili sauce or pepper-flake mixture and 4 tablespoons of the lemon juice. Gently drop

half of the dumplings into the hot liquid and simmer them for 5 minutes. Remove the dumplings with a slotted spoon and set them aside. drop the remaining dumplings into the liquid and simmer them for 5 minutes. When the second batch is done, return the first batch of dumplings to the pan. Heat the dumplings through, then add the melon balls, the salt and the remaining lemon juice. serve the soup in individual bowls.

Shining Noodle Salad with Beef and Tomato

250 g (8 oz) flat cellophane noodles or rice noodles
Two 175 g (6 oz) fillet steaks, trimmed of all fat
60 g (2 oz) red onion, thinly sliced
1 lime, grated rind only
4 tablespoons fresh lime juice
2 teaspoons finely chopped fresh coriander
2 teaspoons very finely chopped fresh lemon grass, or 1^1/$_2$ teaspoons grated lemon rind
2 teaspoons finely chopped fresh mint
^{1}/$_2$ teaspoon finely chopped hot chili pepper, or ^{1}/$_2$ teaspoon sambal oelek
^{1}/$_2$ teaspoon finely chopped garlic
3 tablespoons low-sodium soy sauce or shoyu
1 tablespoon safflower oil
^{1}/$_2$ teaspoon sugar
2 small round lettuces
3 ripe tomatoes, thinly sliced
Mint leaves for garnish

1 Grill the steaks until they are rare and allow them to cool. Cut each steak in half lengthwise. Thinly slice each half into pieces about 3 mm ($^1/_8$ inch) thick, and toss the pieces with the onion slices. Set the mixture aside.

2 In a large bowl, combine the lime rind and juice, coriander, lemon grass or lemon rind, mint, chili pepper or sambal oelek, garlic, soy sauce, oil and sugar. Pour half of this marinade over the beef and onion slices, reserving the other half of the marinade for the noodles. Toss well, then cover the beef and let it marinade for the noodles. Toss well, then cover the beef and let it marinate at room temperature for 30 minutes.

3 Pour enough boiling water over the noodles to cover them. Soak the noodles until they are *al dente* – 10 to 15 minutes, depending on their thickness. Drain the noodles, rinse them in cold water, and drain them once again. Wrap the noodles in a clean towel and squeeze out most of their moisture. Cut the noodles into 15 cm (6 inch) lengths and toss them with the reserved half of the marinade.

4 To serve, arrange some lettuce leaves on each of six plates. At one side of each plate, just inside the edge of the leaves, arrange several tomato slices in a crescent. Mound some noodles next to the tomatoes. Arrange the beef slices on top of the noodles, then distribute the onion strips round the beef in a flower pattern. Garnish the salads with the mint leaves and serve them at room temperature.

1 lemon, cut into wedges (optional)
1 bunch watercress (optional)

1 Pour enough boiling water over the rice noodles to cover them, and let them soak for 15 minutes. In a large bowl, combine the prawns with the lemon grass, ginger, garlic and salt. (If you are using lemon rind in place of lemon grass, set it aside for later use.)

2 Heat 1 tablespoon of the oil in a hot wok or a heavy frying pan over high heat. Add the prawn mixture and stir-fry it until the prawns are barely cooked – about 3 minutes. Transfer to a plate. Reserve any juices left in the wok, then wipe the wok clean.

3 In a saucepan, combine the coconut milk, stock, lemon juice, soy sauce and chili sauce. bring the liquid just to the boil. Heat the remaining oil in the wok Add the coriander and onion, and gently stir-fry them until the onion is limp – about 4 minutes. Add the red pepper and stir-fry the mixture for 1 minute more.

4 Drain the noodles and add them to the red pepper and onion in the wok. Pour in the coconut milk mixture and reserve the juices from the prawns. Cook over medium heat, stirring, until most of the liquid has evaporated. If you are using lemon rind in place of lemon grass, add it now. Stir in the prawns and briefly heat them through. Serve immediately, garnished, if you like, with the lemon wedges and watercress.

Nonya Rice Noodles with Prawns

350 g (12 oz) flat rice noodles
350 g (12 oz) fresh prawns, shelled
2 teaspoons very finely chopped fresh lemon grass, or
    1$^1/_2$ teaspoons freshly grated lemon rind
1 teaspoon very finely chopped fresh ginger root
$^1/_2$ teaspoon very finely chopped garlic
$^1/_2$ teaspoon salt
2 tablespoons safflower oil
125 ml (4 fl oz) unsweetened coconut milk
350 ml (12 fl oz) unsalted chicken stock, reduced to
    $^1/_4$ ltr (8 fl oz)
6 tablespoons fresh lemon juice
2 teaspoons low-sodium soy sauce or shoyu
2 teaspoons sweet chili sauce
2 teaspoons ground coriander
1 large onion, halved lengthwise and thinly sliced
1 sweet red pepper, seeded, deribbed and thinly
    sliced

Nonya rice noodles with prawns.

57

<table>
<tr><td rowspan="2">Menu
3</td><td>**Stir-Fried Pork with Mange-Tout**
Ma Po Szechwan Noodles
Steamed Chinese Cabbage with Green Pepper</td></tr>
</table>

What to drink

A light slightly sweet Australian or New Zealand Semillon would be ideal with this menu.

Start-to-Finish Steps

1 Soak the mushrooms for the pork recipe and assemble ingredients for all three recipes.
2 Follow Szechwan noodles recipe step 1.
3 Follow cabbage recipe steps 1 and 2, and pork recipe step 2. Put water on to boil for noodles.
4 Follow cabbage recipe step 3 and noodles recipe step 2.
5 Follow cabbage recipe step 4 and noodles recipe steps 3 and 4. Keep both warm while you stir-fry pork.
6 Follow pork recipe steps 3 to 6 and serve with noodles and cabbage dish.

Stir-Fried Pork with Mange-Tout

250 g (8 oz) pork fillet, trimmed of fat and cut into 5 mm (¼ inch) thick strips
5 dried shiitake mushrooms, soaked in water for 20 to 30 minutes

Stir-fried pork with mange-tout.

58

12 baby sweetcorn
3 spring onions
2 teaspoons safflower oil
1 garlic clove crushed
1 cm (¹/₂ inch) fresh ginger root, cut into fine julienne
200 g (7 oz) bamboo shoots, thinly sliced lengthwise
200 g (7 oz) mange-tout
1 teaspoon low-sodium soy sauce or shoyu
1 teaspoon dry or medium-dry sherry
2 tablespoons unsalted veal stock or water
1 teaspoon cornflour potato flour, mixed with
    4 teaspoons cold water
1 small carrot, sliced into fine julienne

Sherry Marinade
1 teaspoon low-sodium soy sauce or shoyu
1 teaspoon dry or medium-dry sherry
1 teaspoon cornflour or potato flour
White pepper

1 To prepare the marinade, mix together the soy sauce, sherry, cornflour or potato flour and a little white pepper in a non reactive-dish. Add the pork strips and toss them well to coat them evenly, then leave to marinate for 15 to 20 minutes.

2 Meanwhile, strain the mushroom-soaking liquid and reserve it; squeeze the mushrooms dry and slice them thinly. Blanch the sweetcorn for 5 minutes in a pan of lightly salted boiling water with a squeeze of lemon juice added, then refresh them in cold water and drain. Shred the spring onions finely along the grain and put the strips in a bowl of iced water; when the strips have curled, drain them.

3 Heat 1 teaspoon of the oil in a wok or a large, deep frying pan until it is hot but not smoking, then stir-fry the pork strips over medium-high heat until they are light brown. Remove the pork strips from the wok and drain them in a sieve over a bowl.

4 Wipe the wok clean with paper towels, then heat the remaining oil until smoking and add the garlic. Discard the garlic when brown and add the ginger, bamboo shoots and mushrooms. Stir-fry for 3 minutes, then add the mange-tout and stir-fry for a further 3 minutes.

5 Reduce the heat and add the soy sauce, sherry, stock or water, reserved mushroom-soaking liquid and any meat juices from the pork strips. Increase the heat and cook for another 2 to 3 minutes; then add the cornflour mixture and stir until the sauce thickens and turns translucent. Add the pork strips and the sweetcorn to the wok and heat them through for 1 minute, then remove the wok from the heat and stir in the carrot julienne.

6 Serve the finsihed dish from the wok with the spring onion curls sprinkled over it.

Ma Po Szechwan Noodles

250 g (8 oz) thin, dried wheat noodles or linguine
250 g (8 oz) lean pork, trimmed of all fat and diced
2 teaspoons fermented black beans, rinsed and
    drained
2 tablespoons dry sherry
2 teaspoons finely chopped fresh garlic
4 spring onions, thinly sliced
6 dried shiitake or Chinese black mushrooms, soaked
    in very hot water for 20 minutes, drained,
    stemmed and diced, soaking liquid reserved
2 teaspoons hoisin sauce
2 teaspoons low-sodium soy sauce or shoyu
1 to 2 teaspoons chili paste with garlic
¹/₄ ltr (8 fl oz) unsalted chicken stock, reduced to
    125 ml (4 fl oz)
1 teaspoon cornflour
1 tablespoon safflower oil
¹/₂ teaspoon dark sesame oil

1 Combine the pork with the black beans, sherry, garlic and half of the spring onions. Let the pork marinate for 10 minutes. Meanwhile, in a large saucepan combine the mushrooms, their soaking liquid, the hoisin sauce, soy sauce, chili paste, and all but 1 tablespoon of the reduced chicken stock. heat the mixture to a simmer.

2 Add the noodles to 4 ltrs (7 pts) of boiling water. Start testing after 3 minutes and cook until *al dente*.

3 Drain the noodles and combine them with the stock-and-mushroom mixture. combine the cornflour with the reserved tablespoon of stock. Add this mixture to the noodles and simmer them for 3 minutes.

4 Heat the safflower oil in a hot wok or a deep, heavy frying pan over high heat; add the pork mixture and stir-fry it for about 1 minute. Turn off the heat, add the noodles and sesame oil to the pork mixture, and toss well. Arrange the noodles on a heated serving platter and garnish them with the remaining spring onions.

Steamed Chinese Cabbage with Green Pepper

1 kg (2 lb) Chinese cabbage, thinly sliced
1 teaspoon Szechwan peppercorns, or $\frac{1}{2}$ teaspoon freshly ground black pepper
600 ml (2 fl oz) cider vinegar
1 tablespoon dark brown sugar
$\frac{1}{2}$ teaspoon crushed red pepper flakes
$\frac{1}{4}$ teaspoon salt
1 sweet green pepper, seeeded, deribbbed and thinly sliced

1 In a small, heavy frying pan, toast the Szechwan peppercorns over medium heat for 3 to 4 minutes, shaking the pan frequently. Transfer the peppercorns to a work surface and crush them.

2 Combine the vinegar, brown sugar, Szechwan or black pepper, red pepper flakes, salt and 600 ml (2 fl oz) of water in a small saucepan. Bring the liquid to the boil over high heat, and cook it rapidly to reduce it by half – 4 to 5 minutes. Remove the sauce from the heat and set it aside.

3 Pour enough water into a large pan to fill it about $2\frac{1}{2}$ cm (1 inch) deep. Put a vegetable steamer in the pan and bring the water to the boil. Put the sliced cabbage and green pepper in the steamer, cover the pan tightly, and steam the vegetables until the cabbage is just barely wilted – about 3 minutes.

4 Transfer the vegetables to a serving bowl and pour the sauce through a strainer on to them. Toss the vegetables well and let them stand for 5 minutes before serving.

Meet the Cooks

Ken Hom

Author and cookery teacher, Ken Hom, who now lives in California, began to cook at the age of eleven in his uncle's Chinese restaurant. He often guides culinary tours to Hong Kong, where he also has a cookery school. He is the author of *Chinese Techniques*.

Jane Philips

Jane Philips was converted to Wok cookery at an early stage in her cookery career. A great lover of Chinese food, she has picked up many tips and ideas for her recipe collection from restaurants around the world.

Karen Lee

Karen Lee has been a cookery teacher and caterer for many years and has travelled widely in China to develop her interst in Chinese cooking. She has intoduced a range of Chinese sauces and condiments to speciality shops and is the author of *Chinese Cooking Secrets*.

John Bentley

The owner of a flourishing restaurant on the West coast of the US, John Bentley originally had no thoughts of a cookery career when he first began cooking with a wok. He has visited China several times and greatly admires the variety of regional Chinese cuisines.

Mai Leung

Mai Leung was born in Canton and brought up in Hong Kong. She learned to cook at home, and later studied in Hong Kong with chefs from various regions of China. To enhance her knowledge of regional cuisines, she travelled through China and Taiwan. She is the author of *The Classic Chinese Cook Book* and *Mai Leung's Dim Sum*.

Francis Morton

Francis Morton inherited his love of cooking from his maternal grandmother. Francis uses his skills as a cook to combine the best of both Eastern and Western cooking traditions.

A Wealth of Herbs

Increasingly, herbs are arriving in the markets fresh; the proliferation of health stores and other specialist shops has widened choice, and many cooks with gardens have taken to raising their own. Recent ethnic influences have called attention to once seemingly esoteric herbs. Coriander, for one, is at last gaining deserved popularity. in Europe, although cooks in Asia and the Middle East have been using it for centuries.

Anyone wishing to dry fresh herbs can tie them loosely in a bundle and hang them upside down in a cool, dark, well-ventilated place for several weeks. When the leaves are completely dried, strip them from the stems and store them in an airtight container.

Two swifter methods of preserving herbs make use of the microwave oven and the freezer. To microwave herbs, place five or six sprigs at a time between paper towels and microwave them on high for 1 to 3 minutes until the leaves are brittle. Store the leaves loosely in airtight jars.

To freeze herbs, rinse the sprigs and pat them dry. Strip the leaves off the stems and put them into a heavy-duty plastic bag. Gently flatten the bag to force out the air, seal the bag tightly, and place it in your freezer. Use the leaves as the need arises.

Basil (also called sweet basil): This fragrant herb, with its underlying flavour of anise and hint of clove, goes particularly well with tomato.

Chervil: The small, lacy leaves of this herb have a taste akin to parsley with a touch of anise. It is good in salads and salad dressings. Chervil is popular in France where it is often an ingredient in herb mixtures, including *fines herbes*. When used in cooking, chervil should be added at the end, lest its subtle flavour be lost.

Chives: The smallest of the onions, chives grow in grassy clumps. When finely cut, the hollow leaves contribute their delicate, oniony flavour to fresh salads and raw vegetables. Chives should always be used fresh, as dried ones are virtually tasteless.

Coriander (also called cilantro): The serrated leaves of the coriander plant impart a distinctive fragrance and a flavour that is both mildly sweet and bitter. Coriander leaves should be used fresh or added at the end of cooking if their flavour is to be appreciated fully.

Dill: A sprightly herb with feathery leaves, dill enhances cucumber and many other fresh vegetables, as well as fish and shellfish. When used in cooking, dill should be added towards the end of the process to preserve its delicate flavour. Both dill seeds and dill leaves can be